Endorsements:

"Jeremy Dunlap, along with Danny's parents Dan Dietz and Cindy Dietz-Marsh, gives the arousing portrait of Danny Dietz, a truly great American who personifies triumph over adversity, courage under fire, and love of both family and country. This is a must read for anyone who enjoys the freedoms of being an American."

—Peter Berg, Director of The Lone Survivor

"Jeremy Dunlap has captured the voice and experiences of Danny Dietz Jr. and his fellow SEALs, far from home and facing the possibility of mortal danger at any given moment. This gripping account of the life of a military hero is a tribute to the dedication and devotion of the SEALs, and all who have bravely worn the uniform of the United States."

—Texas Governor Rick Perry

"Time and time again after hearing about incredible acts of valor exhibited by young men and women in our military we ask ourselves. 'where do we get such people?' When you read the story of Danny Deitz and his family, the answer becomes clear. We get them from loving parents who teach their children the meaning of personal responsibility. We get them from families wherein the love of one's country is engrained. In short, we get them from the soul of America. I for one, thank God for them."

—Tom Tancredo, Former Congressman

This wonderful book not only depicts the life and heroic actions of Danny in such a unique way but also asks us all of us Americans, "How can we be inspired by DJ's story and improved by his example, making an impact in this life and leaving a legacy that others will remember?

—Phil Taylor, Artist and Founder of the American Fallen Soldiers Project

DANNY

THE VIRTUES WITHIN

LARRY:
WE LIVE BECAUSE
OF FREEDOM!
Jer

"NEVER FORGET"
MY SON
Cpl Dt Mc

For My Son

Don

DANNY

THE VIRTUES WITHIN

What America Can Learn
from Navy SEAL Danny Dietz

Jeremy Dunlap

with Dan Dietz
and Cindy Dietz-Marsh

As seen in the Motion Picture
Lone Survivor

WINTERS
PUBLISHING GROUP

Published by Winters Publishing
2448 E. 81st St.
Suite #4802
Tulsa, OK 74137

Book Design Copyright 2014 by Winters Publishing. All rights reserved.
Cover design by Maca Ferguson with Errol Villamante
Interior design by Joana Quilantang

Published in the United States of America

ISBN: 978-1-62902-536-0
Biography & Autobiography / Military
13.12.13

Contents

Acknowledgments from the Author:
First and foremost, I must acknowledge my Lord and Savior Jesus Christ. The Author of virtue, grace, and life. I also have to mention the incredible amount of trust that Cindy Dietz-Marsh and Dan Dietz placed in me. It has been an honor. As well, I must acknowledge all the work my mother, Dr. Linda Dunlap, put into proofreading of and suggestions for this manuscript. Without her, the editing phase of this project would have taken much longer. To those who have asked to remain anonymous, your unending advice and support have been crucial. Finally, to my wife Christina, my daughters Kaylynn and Madeline, I love you.

Acknowledgments from Dan Dietz and Cindy Dietz - Marsh
Dan Dietz and Cindy Dietz-Marsh want to acknowledge Naval Special Warfare, Admiral Pybus, and Steve Gilmore for their help in this project. Phil Taylor, whose lifelike portrait in so many ways brought our son home was such an encouragement and critical in the introduction to Jeremy. Special thanks to Maca Ferguson who took a book cover concept and brought it together. As well, we must thank Lieutenant Commander Jon Schaffner for his unending support and care. We would be remiss to not thank the many family, friends, and Americans from around the globe who have poured out their care, support, and prayers.

Dedication from Dan Dietz and Cindy Dietz-Marsh
In loving honor of our son and brother, Danny. He will forever be our hero and warrior. We love and miss you every minute of every hour of every day till we become a family again in the heavens above.

Dedication from the Author:
Danny, though we never met this side of Heaven, your warrior mentality is everything I long for my life to encompass. To all warriors, because you are brave, we continue to be free. God bless you and this great nation in which you serve.

Foreword

When I look back at my tenure as Secretary of the Navy, I often reflect on the different perspective it gave me on matters that extend well beyond our Navy and Marine Corps. That perspective provided me with a number of learning experiences that I value deeply. Perhaps the most profound lesson concerns the broad dimension of human beliefs and behaviors. From the terrorists that regard innocent men, women and children as legitimate targets to the SEALs and other Special Forces personnel who take great personal risks to protect all of us, the extreme differences in behavior are self evident. What lies behind those differences is, however, far more complex, and not well understood.

Much has been written about Al Qaeda and other terrorist organizations, their recruiting and training techniques, and the individuals that they employ.

Ongoing reporting from news agencies has also provided us with an appreciation for the societal support that terrorists receive. All of this has been consumed by a public trying to comprehend what motivates terrorists to target the innocent in acts such as the Lockerbie bombing or the attacks of 9/11.

Far less is known or appreciated regarding those who volunteer for our Special Forces, such as the SEALs. For the most part, recent writings have focused on the SEAL's exploits and heroic acts, from Operation Red Wings in the Hindu Kush Mountains of Afghanistan to the killing of

Usama Bin Laden in Pakistan. Much has also been written about the physical challenges of SEAL training and the extraordinary standards of fitness they must maintain. However, my interactions with the SEAL community have led me to believe that it is their character which stands out most clearly and, more so than their physical capabilities, enables them to accomplish the incredible missions they take on. Furthermore, I see that character reflected in their families, their parents and their spouses, leading me to suspect that any story regarding our SEALs must start with the story of their upbringing.

I first met Cindy and Dan Dietz, along with the Axelsons, when their sons' posthumous Navy Crosses were presented at the Navy Memorial in DC in September of 2006. The emotion of that event, just 15 months after the loss of their sons, cannot be overstated, yet the character of the families shined through their pain.

I subsequently got to meet and develop a longstanding relationship with the parents of Michael Murphy and other members of the Operation Red Wings community, families of both SEALs and Nightstalkers. Not surprisingly, I have found that the character of these families is consistently evident, reflecting on the character of their sons.

A commonly asked question about heroes such as those lost in Operation Red Wings is "Where do we get such men?" That question is as applicable today as it was in 1954 when those same words were spoken at the end of the movie, "The Bridges at Toko-Ri." We get them from communities such as Littleton CO, Cupertino CA and Patchogue NY, raised by families who instilled in them a sense of character that, more than any other attribute, led to their heroic acts, on behalf of their team and our nation.

Jeremy Dunlap has written a book that is a study in the development of character. It is a book that tells the story of Danny Dietz and how he found his way to the Hindu Kush. Equally important, it tells the story of the Dietz family, their community and the maturation of Danny Dietz. It is not a story of a "perfect" child or family, whatever the definition of perfect might be. It is, however, a story that rings true and helps explain how Danny developed into the man of character that he became.

There was a time when stories of men such as Danny Dietz were taught in school; when classrooms had many biographies, often focusing on the early years of great Americans. That is what I recall of my early education. I don't see that focus today, and that is most unfortunate. We need to tell the story of all that is good in our country and how the people we call heroes helped to make it that way. Dunlap's book is a good step in that direction.

—Donald Winter
74th Secretary of the Navy (2006-2009)

It's Time

Almost immediately after Danny's death it became apparent that the public was interested in what kind of kid, teenager and young man he was. It became more apparent during TV and radio interviews when we could almost count on the question being asked in one form or another.

At one point Danny's Dad and I said we need to put DJ's story out there in writing. We had no idea where to start or what to do, or if we could even tell the story. His death was still fresh in our minds and even talking about him was very painful. He was never out of our thoughts. We put the thought of a book out of our minds for several years.

Then about a year ago we decided it was time. That's the time Jeremy Dunlap came into our lives. Right from our first meeting with Jeremy we knew he would be the one to guide us on the journey.

Without any real previous conversation, Jeremy told us what we had been thinking all along. It's time for the world to find out what kind of childhood this American hero had. We had to tell the good times as well as the bad times. What made him stand out among his peers? What had been instilled in him to drive him to excel in Navy SEAL BUDS training? The more we talked the more excited we became and eager to start.

And now here we are. Danny Sr. and I believe this book will fulfill our quest of sharing our son and his virtues with the world.

-Cindy Dietz-Marsh

Prologue

Hallowed Ground

"Take off your sandals, for the place where you are standing is holy ground."[1]

Surely I was standing on holy ground. Gone was my natural comedian persona, and in its place was a deep sense of reverence. Here I stood in front of a Gold Star mother, a woman who has earned that title because she has lost a child to the perils of war. A Gold Star mother is a unique and special person who carries within her a deep burden often masked behind the smile and face of normality. She knows, deep inside her soul, she raised a child—to die in battle. Not only to die but to give his life—for her very freedom. Her steps are consecrated by the blood of a son who gave his life for the sake of his team, for the sake of America. That is amazing.

As my wife and I shook Cindy Dietz-Marsh's hand, I felt as though I should loosen the strings and remove my shoes, as we were standing on holy ground. Here stood a woman, who with her husband, through many prayers, tears, and even frustrations had given America a hero. We had come to discuss with the family a potential book detailing the life of Danny Dietz, Navy SEAL.

As we walked up the driveway with Cindy, I saw Phil Taylor, co-founder of the American Fallen Soldier Project standing on the porch. Phil has a heart as big as his beloved state of Texas. Tall, lanky, full of life, and never meeting a stranger, Phil, along with his wife Lisa, honor the fallen warrior with portraits so lifelike that numerous families have felt as though their warrior indeed came home. He stood there with that big toothy grin, motioning us up the steps. Phil had been the connecting point between the Dietz family and me.

There was only one word to describe this entire moment: humbling.

As I walked through the front door of Cindy's house, I felt the oxygen pushed out of my lungs as I saw smaller prints of a Danny Dietz portrait painted by Phil. The weight of Danny's legacy fell hard on me. We began walking around the living room, examining the reminders, other paintings, pictures, the accolades, and the gear of this fallen warrior. Cindy Dietz, Danny's mother, began to recount different stories of Danny, who she still calls DJ, a boyhood nickname.

For a brief moment I envied young Petty Officer Dietz who will forever, at the age of twenty-five, be frozen in time. I envied the tenacity, the steadfastness of that SEAL ethos of which I had only read, never lived. I envied that which was deep in him, common to all Navy SEALs, that virtue that seemingly Hollywood can glorify but never explain. I looked at the famous picture of Danny crouching in the desert sand, eyes squinting. For a brief moment I felt that his steely eyes were staring back at me—straight through me. It seemed as though he was saying, "I don't need a book about me. But if you're the writer—don't mess it up. Don't make me bigger than I was."

Got it, Danny.

After some initial conversation, we piled into cars and drove the short distance to the apartment of Dan Dietz Sr. A striking resemblance to his son Danny, Dan Sr. opened the front screen door of his apartment, welcoming us in. As he began to talk about his son, his resolute eyes hinted at the loss he still so deeply felt. The small apartment living room was covered from floor to ceiling with tributes and reminders of the fallen SEAL; never a day passes without regret or without a longing to simply see him—one more time.

"Danny was brave," Dan Sr. said to me in a tone that displayed the honor he holds for his son. "He wasn't scared of a thing, a thing. That boy…" His words trailed off as if he suddenly had left the room and was visiting another place. "I wish I had half the virtue, half the courage that boy had."

Later that evening, after returning to Cindy's home, Dan Sr. shared with me something that for the rest of my life will shutter my soul.

"I wish Danny would have run." With his Kansas-rooted brusque voice he looked me in the eye and continued. "I don't mind saying that. I wish the moment the Taliban hit 'em, he would have run. But I know better. Danny didn't run. He wouldn't have run. That wasn't Danny. The only way he would have run was right up that hill into them, the Taliban."

As Dan Sr. spoke those words, for a brief moment my mind returned to images I first conjured up, first visualized, when I had read the only available firsthand account of the June 28, 2005 portion of Operation Red Wings in *The Lone*

Survivor by Marcus Luttrell. I sat in an airport, highlighting every mention Luttrell made of Danny Dietz. I wept. My tears were a constant pulling of my soul between sadness and anger. I kept thinking, once saying out loud, "Come on, guys, left flank, and right flank, left—" I squinted with pain as Danny took hit by hit, bullet by bullet. I shook my head with disbelief as each time I pictured that Navy SEAL taking a deep breath, shaking off the pain, and pulling that weapon back to his shoulder. I could see him. In my mind, in my heart I could see Danny. As the book calls him, "that lion?" just wouldn't stop.

Those images have never left.

My attention was snapped back to the conversation at hand, as Cindy, who had earlier left the living room, returned from the back hallway. There were tears in her eyes. I figured the tears to be the continuing sadness of a parent who had buried her son. This time I was wrong. She held out her hand. A hand that had once held a baby boy, patched the wounded knee of a toddler cowboy, and hugged an adolescent who swore he was going to be a Navy SEAL—held something out. It was a challenge coin, honoring her fallen son. I knew that these special coins were only given in times of recognition as a special honor to someone who may have known Danny Dietz or did something to pay tribute to his memory. Few of the challenge coins, medallions, have been made, and I am sure many would covet the moment to simply hold one.

I took the medallion sized challenge coin from her hand, and there he was, Danny Dietz, molded in silver, armed to the teeth, standing on alert. The medallion bore the image of the Navy SEAL trident, Danny's BUD/S class number 232, an image of the Navy Cross, and wrapped around the edges were the words "SDVT 2, Never Forget."

I flipped the medallion over to see another image of the SEAL trident and the words, in all capitals, "IN MEMORY OF OUR FALLEN BROTHERS." I looked at that medallion in total silence.

Cindy spoke, "Jeremy, I want you to have this. So our angel can watch over you as you write about our angel. Through the years we have had authors approach us, people asking if we will ever do a book. We believe the time is now, and you're the guy to write it."

I sat there speechless. Once again the oxygen was pushed from my lungs, sucked out of the room. I could hardly speak as I stared down at the medallion. I looked back up, across the couch at my wife, then across the room to Phil, and then my eyes rested on Dan Sr. There was not a dry eye in the room.

I looked back again to my wife as she said, "They are asking you, honey—you—to write the book."

I stared back down at the medallion. This would be a moment I would never forget. This medallion would mark a moment in my life, forever.

—◄╱╿╲►—

In his dedication of the National Cemetery at Gettysburg, President Abraham Lincoln in his short address that has been enshrined for the ages said:

> The world will little note, nor long remember what we say here, but it can never forget what

they did here. *It is for us the living, rather, to be dedicated here to the unfinished work which they who fought here have thus far so nobly advanced.* It is rather for us to be here dedicated to the great task remaining before us—that from these honored dead we take increased devotion to that cause for which they gave the last full measure of devotion—*that we here highly resolve that these dead shall not have died in vain*—that this nation, under God, shall have a new birth of freedom—and that government of the people, by the people, for the people, shall not perish from the earth. (emphasis added)[3]

I truly believe the best way to honor the fallen warrior, to honor Danny Dietz, is to recommit our lives to the simple values they so dearly upheld. These simple values are the very moral fabric of the freedom to which we Americans so deeply value. And in that moment of recommitment, we must put action to word, motion to emotion. This book is written with that goal in mind.

This is a different kind of Navy SEAL book. There are no mentions of major military operations. There are no harrowing battle scenes. There is not necessarily any of the cool stuff that is the essence of Hollywood. I too have read a lot of those books. I love those books. We need those books. Yet, this is not one of those books. In addition, there are no stories to embellish a legacy that quite frankly needs no embellishment. They are stories of a kid turned adolescent who demonstrated a virtue worthy of the elite Navy SEALs. This is a book of essays focused on the values of an American hero, his community, and what we as his countrymen can learn from such goodness. This is not a self-help book; this is a contemplative book reminding us that the greatest way to honor the fallen is by living lives worthy of their sacrifice. And when we live such lives, we bolster the very liberty for which they fought.

Each chapter of the book ends with a brief "Medallion Moment," summarizing final thoughts, opinions, and hopes for us personally and a nation as a whole. Following the "Medallion Moment" are lines of empty space. Maybe for you it will be a place to write a few thoughts, create your own ethos, or jot down some changes to be made in your life as a result of his stories that would bring honor to our fallen warrior. The heart and goal of writing this book is that lives may be made better, even different. That is what happened in my medallion moment, sitting in Cindy's living room. That is what has happened to numerous people who have already heard the different stories of this Navy SEAL.

To this day, that medallion sits in my suit pocket and travels with me all over the nation. Few people, until now, have known this. It is a constant reminder of the warrior I long to become, the warrior I will be. It encourages me that there are still men of virtue, men of honor. And when I stand in front of people to offer training and development solutions or a motivational moment, it helps reassure me that someday, somewhere, I will be standing to speak about the freedom, about the nation that Danny Dietz so dearly loved. I too will fight the battle of freedom, my own way.

In the other pocket is a military challenge coin, presented by a group of guys who also made a lasting impact on my heart. If they are reading they know who they are.

Gentlemen—and I use that term loosely—long live the little red dot.

Finally, *America needs to read and hear the stories of a boy nicknamed DJ who became Navy SEAL Danny Dietz.* Today, many are desperately searching for heroes. We are in need of hope and belief that there still exists "a few good men, to turn back the wrong of night." We want to learn from their steps, their mistakes, and sit as close as we can to the glowing light of a virtue (or virtues) we so long for ourselves and those who hold leadership over us. Like never before, if I may quote the nineties rock group, we "need something to believe in."[4]

If you are in search of a hero, look no further. Danny Dietz embodied the qualities for which we have long searched. His community has a moral fabric that runs deep, and he was a perfect fit. His actions dictated a courage beyond human reason, humility beyond our comprehension, intelligence that marveled a genius, and service, always service before self. He gave, lived, and yes, even died for his team. This special man had a never-quit steadfastness only matched by an integrity that dictated to always do right by thy fellow man. This is the stuff of legends. Danny's stories stand alone based on character—no embellishments added, no additives needed. As you read, you will be reminded of the greatness of the America Danny Dietz so deeply loved.

This is a glimpse, only a glimpse into what drove this American warrior. For some, my prayer is that you will find affirmation of that fighter within. For others, I pray that you will discover or uncover your seemingly lost warrior, which resides deep in the virtue within.

Section One

Courage When We Need It Most

"Courage is not simply one of the virtues but the form of every virtue at the testing point, which means at the point of highest reality." C.S Lewis[5]

Essay One: A Calling to be Courageous

Why do we as humans settle? Here is what I mean. You ask any seven-year-old, "What do you want to be when you grow up?"

They do not answer, "When I grow up I want to settle for a paycheck, complain about my boss, and take vacations with noisy kids that ultimately wear me out."

No. They tell you that they want to be a fireman, police officer, a teacher, a doctor, and so forth. One time I asked my oldest daughter, when she was the ripe age of three, "K-bugg, what do you want to be when you grow up?"

Her response, "Dadda, I wanna be a hippopotamus."

I simply said that her mother and I would do everything in our power to help her become the best hippopotamus she could be.

There is an unofficial biblical passage that celebrates the call of courage for special operation forces. It is taken from the call of the Prophet Isaiah. In the passage, the soon-to-be-prophet is approached by the Holy One and given a charge. Now if you read the entire book of Isaiah, you learn of the hardships, the doubts, the wonderings, and the struggles of this famous prophet. He was courageous. And his courageous work, speeches, and stances began with ten simple yet grand words from God himself:

Whom shall I send? And who will go for us?[6]

In five words, Isaiah quickly responded, "Here am I! Send me!"[7]

Called to courage, Isaiah answered in the affirmative. Let's not forget, he could have answered in the negative. If you know the Bible, that guy named Jonah was called to courage, and he answered in the negative. (Of course, if you remember the story, he also became the first recorded underwater delivery vehicle pilot, earning a trip in a big fish. Now I am digressing.) It's one thing to have a calling to courage. It's another thing to actually answer and follow the path.

It seems that Danny Dietz was always clear on his calling, his dream: to be a warrior. It feels as though he was called at a young age through his innocent desire and innocent longing to be a cowboy. Later this calling to courage, to be a warrior, was manifested through his desire to become a ninja. Once he realized becoming a ninja was not possible for him, he set his middle school eyes on becoming: a Navy SEAL. The calling of a warrior, to be of courage, never let go of Danny Dietz.

Through adolescence Danny often spoke of his warrior-minded calling in life. On one occasion, writing to a friend, it appears that he may have believed his life would very well be cut short. Whether or not Danny Dietz somehow knew that someday his courage enacted, his justice exacted, would potentially cost him his life, we will probably never know. However, with his life he demonstrated that which America so badly needs reminding of today: a calling to courage.

Essay Two: A Kidlike Bravery

He wanted a punching bag. Danny Dietz, at the age of four, wanted a punching bag! I wanted one of those miniature, remote control racetracks with the red-and-blue race cars. Like me, you probably were not thinking of a punching bag. The problem was: he was four years old. In 1984 it was difficult to locate such an item for a four-year-old boy. On a side note, racetracks were a dime a dozen. With already two years of experience, he loved the martial arts. After spending countless hours watching Dad perfect his moves and train others in the art of Tae Kwon Do, he wanted a punching bag. According to DJ, his Christmas gift request would help him "work on his moves." I simply wanted to make turn two and keep the little plastic yellow car on the track.

As the holiday season approached, Cindy Dietz searched every store she could to locate toddler-sized punching bags. Not surprisingly, no such product existed. On the suggestion from a retail clerk at a sporting goods store, Cindy turned her efforts to the idea of a bop bag. Shaped like a bowling pin, the inflatable bop bag bearing the images of Bugs Bunny and Daffy Duck could take a hit and then bounce right back stationary.

Perfect.

Now all parents know it is one thing for a child to want a toy. It is another thing for the child to play with that toy on a regular basis past Christmas day. As parents we all have witnessed a child laughing with joy as they open a gift, only moments later to be playing with the paper, the box, or an ornament hanging from the Christmas tree. That would not be the case of four-year-old DJ. In fact, Bugs and Daffy had no idea what was in store for them. Once inflated, DJ seemingly could not get enough "practice" on his "punching bag." Hours passed hours, and Cindy's son would be found kicking, punching, and blocking the vicious blows of the bunny and duck. After much time passed, DJ's love of that bop bag did not fade.

He was the born warrior. Little to her understanding, by purchasing that toddler-sized punching bag, Cindy seemingly fostered her son's innate spirit. As an adolescent, as a SEAL, the courage to fight, to stand may have seemed like a natural thing for Danny. And while there is no doubt he had some sort of special, innate courage, his embracing of the journey to such a virtue began as a four-year-old boy—hitting Bugs Bunny and Daffy Duck.

As typical for DJ, he took the "punching bag" experience one step further. He enjoyed chasing other students around the Tae Kwon Do studio. Chasing boys much older and larger than him, DJ could be heard yelling, "Come on, and spar with me!"

Dan Sr. recalled the story with laughter. "I remember it, because I would be trying to get class started, and there would go DJ, running at full speed, chasing another kid across the room. And typically the kid would be older and bigger then DJ, but the older kid would be running like crazy to get away from him."

Right or wrong, kid-like bravery has little concern for potential consequences of courage. Kid-like bravery seemingly squelches the voices of hesitation, pushing past the warnings of risk, and simply says what needs to be said, does what needs to be done. Kid-like bravery in children makes parents blush, role their eyes, smile at other parents in pain, or simply throw their hands up. Kid-like bravery in adults—makes them heroes. People we admire who exemplify kid-like bravery refused to sit at the back of the bus, ran into the burning World Trade Center Towers, and stood on the frontline protecting others, giving us a reason to keep believing.

Essay Three: The Depth of Courage

America is a culmination of numerous pictures of courage. The "home of the brave" has always celebrated "pictures" of valor with names we know like Rosa Parks or Neil Armstrong. We marvel in humble disbelief over stories of those charging into burning towers, of first responders or warriors running not from the danger but storming headlong into the peril.

And when those leaders in front of us—political, faith, or business—seemingly fail us—our search for these pictures of raw courage becomes that much more desperate. Like a nomad furiously in search of water in a wilderness, with great thirst we pursue any hint of courage albeit an entertainment avenue, a news story, or places of worship. As

Americans, these pictures of courage matter greatly to us as we know in our hearts, in our heart of hearts, that courage is the foundation for so much of that which we believe concerning freedom.

Winston Churchill, former British Prime Minister who from a bunker bravely led Britain against Hitler's impounding Nazis, once said:

> Courage is rightly esteemed the first of human qualities because it is the quality which guarantees all others.[8]

In short, to execute the values of freedom we Americans understand that it takes guts; it takes courage. All the other virtues that we as a nation embrace—such as generosity, life, liberty, the pursuit of happiness, and so forth—hinge on actualization through courage. We have always understood Churchill's words as pure gospel. This virtue is woven deep into our moral fabric, because the great American experiment is based upon people, a brave people.

I pondered this virtue of bravery on an airplane ride to Coronado, California. I was traveling there for one reason: to speak with individuals of NSW (Naval Special Warfare) about this book project to honor a great American warrior, Danny Dietz. After some initial introductions and the first meetings of the morning, I was offered a short tour of a famed facility that turns boys to men and men into Navy SEALs. Humbled beyond words by the experience, I did not see where warriors are made. No, I witnessed a place where courage is enacted so that at some point, when most needed, justice can be exacted. Following the quick tour, I met with a naval captain who has asked to remain nameless. We briefly talked about the book project, Danny Dietz, and Navy SEAL training.

This hero of a man, who clearly lives the SEAL ethos to which he has sworn, asked a pointed question: "Jer, as an outsider, let me ask you this. Why is it we [SEALs] have become such the center of limelight? Why is it that so many people want to know so much about us?"

Without thinking, I answered directly from the heart. "Sir, at a time when Americans were looking for heroes, for courage, you all appeared—and we, the American people, have not forgotten it. With all the lacking in political leadership, we desperately needed someone to believe in, someone to stand in the gap. The Navy SEALs happened to be there at the right—or wrong, depending on how you view it—time."

Seldom do my own words, the words I offer, stick with me. Yet ever since that day, I have returned numerous times to the answer I offered the captain. For in a time when so many things in the country are seemingly going wrong, we Americans long for those pictures of courage to emerge so that we can be reminded that America, the great experiment, is far from over. We want those pictures so that we can sit back, breath, and think to ourselves, *We have not even begun to fight.*

Here in America we will probably never face a battle as daunting or challenging as the battles that Danny Dietz encountered and his brothers continue to encounter. However, we must know from where we derive our source of courage. For some it is a person; for others it may be a story, a hero, or a moment in their own life in which they overcame difficult circumstances. For me personally, and I can only speak for me personally, I have to return to the faith of my childhood. The stories of Scripture remind me that courage exacted is only one prayer away.

For Danny, it is impossible for us to know what his thoughts were during any military operation. However, I cannot help but wonder if more than a few times he did not cling to words similar to that which constructs the Navy SEAL ethos:

> I persevere and thrive on adversity. My Nation expects me to be physically harder and mentally stronger than my enemies. If knocked down, I will get back up, every time.

Essay Four: Courage Begets Sacrifice

Spending numerous years and countless moments witnessing the virtue of courage, Dr. Donald C. Winter gives us an insight into two important aspects (one we will discuss here; another one we will cover in a later essay) of this foundational virtue. Serving as secretary of the United States Navy, Dr. Winter stood in the Colorado sunshine on July 4th, 2007 to dedicate a statue honoring Gunner's Mate Second Class Danny Dietz. In dedicating the monument, the naval secretary declared the following:

> Today we honor the kind of patriot whom the founders would have been immensely proud of and would have extolled as a guardian of their hard-won achievement. Gunner's Mate Second Class Danny Dietz was with us for only twenty-

five years. But Danny's short life was touched with greatness.

He had an irrepressible spirit—and courage, and inner strength, and a devotion to the warrior ethos.

Did you catch that? In the sunshine of that summer day, the navy secretary compared Danny to America's founding fathers. There are very few who would argue against the notion that our forefathers were courageous. However, a little Google search and you will find many of those who signed the great Declaration of Independence, declaring our freedom from a tyrant, paid a great sacrifice. Greatness will always be a painful bi-product of courage. For courage will always beget sacrifice.

Yet I have a gut feeling, and it's only a gut feeling, but I think I am right on this: heroes such as Danny and our many other fallen warriors would have no regrets. I am reminded of the story of son of a very wealthy man who chose to not inherit the riches of his family's business and instead be a missionary, serving the people of a third-world region. He suffered many hardships as a result of his courageous decision. And finally, as a young man, he contracted a local virus and laid on his deathbed, thousands of miles away from home. After his death, his written words concerning his brave decision became public. The response of this young missionary echoes through the hearts of any warrior:

No reserves.

No retreat.

No regrets.[9]

If I had one chance to sit with Danny Dietz in the heaven beyond this world, I believe, I know his response would be exactly the same: "No return. I would never retreat. And I have no regrets." The only difference, he would add a famous SEAL "Hooyah."

Essay Five: Refusing to Hesitate

Have you ever been scared, I mean really scared? Probably. I know I have. I have had moments in which I simply knew that what was about to happen was, "going to sting a little." In those moments did I, did you, lack courage because you had fear? Hardly.

Are some people born with more courage than others? I think so. Don't ask me the science or the studies, but it would appear that some individuals simply have—more courage. Can the virtue of courage be instilled in the young, shaped and molded? Absolutely.

The previously mentioned SEAL captain shared with me that he was thankful for the mothers of Navy SEALs. "Don't get me wrong, the fathers play a role too. But there is something special about a warrior's mother. They have given these men the needed virtue—not me."

Dr. Winter, in the previously mentioned, speech maintained:

> The people who knew him best—those with whom he served, those who grew up alongside him, and *those who molded his character along the way in this very community*—were not surprised that Danny was able to reach the greatest heights

before his life was cut short by a terrorist enemy. They were not surprised that the navy saw in him something that they saw too—that here was a young man who had a special, rare quality that separated him from his peers. (emphasis added)

Courage can be molded. But it would seem that there are some people who maintain a special gifting to push fear aside and make steps that many others would never ponder.

At a young age Danny Dietz seemingly had the raw seeds of courage: lack of fear. Risk and nerve were never a problem as a young boy. He simply never hesitated.

"He was always pushing the limits," Cindy would later recall. "He walked at nine months, and not much later he would scale his crib, crawl down the other side, and take off. I was so afraid he was going to get hurt. DJ had no fear."

On one occasion a terrible thunderstorm hit with ferocious thunder and lighting, leading to an all out hailstorm. As a young boy I myself remember being scared of thunderstorms. Isn't that normal? Yet during this horrific storm, three-year-old DJ came running into the living room and simply proclaimed to his mother, without any sign of concern, that it was "snowballing" outside, referring to the large hail. Could these moments be the seeds of courage?

There were numerous occasions that Cindy wished her son had a little more caution, if not outright fear. Some of those occasions occurred when she looked directly out her kitchen window. Three-year-old DJ loved the tire swing his dad had constructed in the back yard.

As soon as Dan Sr. would come home from work, DJ would meet him in the drive way with a greeting: "Daddy, swing me!"

Tired and dirty from a long day's work of manual labor, young Dan Sr. would take the toddler around to the back yard, put him in the tire swing, and push his son back and forth. Cindy would watch from the kitchen window as the pushes from Dan Sr. grew in momentum.

About the time she would begin to worry that DJ was going to get hurt or become scared, the toddler would let out a huge yell, "Higher, Daddy, higher!" That was Danny.

Dan Sr. shared with me that Danny "always wanted to swing higher, climb anything in his way, or jump from the top step." While fear is one of the several emotions we all hold, pushing the limits, without acknowledging fear, was a natural mode of operation for young DJ. For the special gifting of Danny Dietz, of any special operator, is not that they lack fear. The gift is their repeat ability to push the fear aside, to accept the potential consequences, and to make the decision to step into any situation in which they find themselves.

Essay Six: Courage Defends

A bully is not courageous. A bully is a bully. Courageous people make a stand and do an action that gives to those in need or those in around them. A bully who lives for their own thrills just needs—as we say where I grew up—a whoopin'. Danny Dietz would do just that.

During his middle school years, DJ found out that his younger brother Eric had been the victim of a bullying incident. Uh, oh. This sort of injustice could not be allowed. DJ began to spread the word to every kid he could find that if anyone in the school messed with his kid brother again—it would be bad news for them. That takes courage. What if several kids decided to take DJ up on his challenge? What if he was outnumbered? I highly doubt that this young warrior thought through or even cared about those potentials. All he knew was that justice must be exacted, and his kid brother needed his help.

On one other occasion, according to a family member, the two toughest guys in DJ's high school decided to challenge him to a standoff. They challenged the future warrior to meet them in the local park. He did.

Now let's push the pause button on the narrative for just one moment. If you have ever seen the movie *Tombstone*, you will understand this reference. Near the end of the blockbuster western, Johnny Ringo, a seething villain, challenges the hero Wyatt Earp to a dual. Along with his best friend Doc Holiday, Wyatt Earp knows he cannot defeat the fast-drawing, gun-slinging Johnny Ringo. As the appointed time for the dual arrives, Johnny Ringo walks up a hill to the chosen location for the gunfight. He sees a man standing there waiting and assumes him to be Wyatt Earp. Ringo is wrong.

Pulling his Stetson up above his eyes, Doc Holiday reveals his identity and utters the famous phrase, "Why Johnny Ringo, you look like somebody just walked over your grave."

Ringo knows *he* cannot beat the infamous Doc Holiday.

Now let's return to our story about Danny. As the appointed fight and a modern-day dual commenced, I wonder if the two high school punks squaring off against the future Navy SEAL felt much like Johnny Ringo, like somebody had just walked over their grave. With ease, Danny Dietz took both of them down. By the way, his reason for accepting the challenge in the first place: he had warned the two bullies to cease their pestering of a few high school kids. They refused and challenged DJ to a fight. Like Wyatt Earp, those pestered students could not fight the battle alone. Like Doc Holiday, Danny could. I told you he'd whoop some bullies. And this would not be the only time. Over and over, Danny would enact courage to exact justice.

With the above stories in mind, it is interesting to note that the name Danny translated means *the judge*. Over the last several years, numerous stories have emerged of Danny exacting justice, stepping into situations on behalf of others. Students with which he attended school have shared narratives of Danny Dietz defending or standing up for them. He simply could not stand by when others were being bullied, demeaned, or treated unjustly. As though his very name was a calling, it was seemingly part of his DNA to exact justice.

Essay Seven: A Life of Courage

None of these essays, this book as a whole, is meant to be the panacea, the beginning and the end, on the virtues of which it contains. However, as I began to write this essay

I pondered the other essays and stories of Danny's courage. A life of courage, courage when we need it most, is found in the essay summaries:

A Calling to be Courageous
*Knowing in the end, no matter the outcome you were
called to, born for this moment,*

A Kid-like Bravery
to act without concern for personal consequence,

The Depth of Courage
digging deep to your Source,

Courage Begets Sacrifice
willing to sacrifice all,

Refusing to Hesitate
willing to push past fear,

Courage Defends
for the sake of others

Knowing in the end, no matter the outcome you were called to, born for this moment, to act without concern for personal consequence, digging deep to your Source, willing to sacrifice all, willing to push past fear, for the sake of others. Take that developed sentence and multiply it by numerous occasions, and truly you find a life of bravery. So let us not exemplify Danny or any other fallen hero solely based upon their death. One teammate, and I am summarizing, declared that the men of Operation Red Wings were not heroes because of death, but how well they lived. According to the teammate, though Danny understood the danger of his job, he was always the first one to jump in.[10]

It's not his death, but Danny's life from which we draw such pictures of courage. Whether it is his first grand steps as a toddler in a Tae Kwon Do studio to his stealth movement as a Navy SEAL, he lived a life of daring valor. That brings us full circle back to the closing words of Admiral Winter's speech that day in Colorado:

> Despite his injuries, the warrior in him—his irrepressible spirit—would not allow him to take leave of the field of battle.

Greatness is clearly a byproduct of courage. Yet this hero, along with many others, achieved greatness not by his death, not just by his actions, but by the foundational virtue of courage that was anchored deep in his soul. A hero who exemplified the fourth stanza of the national anthem:

> Oh! thus be it ever, when freemen shall stand
>   Between their loved home and the war's desolation!

A life of courage is life well lived.

Essay Eight: When Courage is Not Enough

I return to the story of Coronado, California, ground zero for Navy SEAL training. During my tour of the famed facility I stood there in awkward silence staring at the "grinder." Covered in detail via several books written by former silent professionals, the grinder is for many a sacred ground. Stew Smith on the military.com website defined the grinder in the following manner:

> The definition of "grinder" is the concrete-asphalt area at BUD/S where the students do their calisthenics workouts. It is surrounded by pull-up bars, dip bars, and the instructors, training officer, and commanding officer's offices. You have the constant feeling of always being watched while you are on the "grinder."[11]

As I stood on the back end of the pavement, I lacked courage. I simply could not, out of respect and honor, walk across the portion of the grinder bearing row after row of painted footprints in the shapes of diving fins. I stood there, frozen for a moment, as if my feet had sunk deep into the pavement. I looked at the infamous brass bell, rung only by those who no longer can handle the physical and mental pressures of BUD/S. Who can blame them?

I looked back down at the diving fin prints, still unable to bring myself to walk across them. For me, I had not earned the right of passage to stand in those footprints. I imagined a few friends of mine, for me, true pictures of courage. They had stood there. I pictured Danny, caught on a YouTube video during BUD/S with a smirk smile. He stood there. I thought of the other three SEALs from Operation Red Wings, the SEALs who had boarded the doomed CH-47 that flew in to rescue Danny and his teammates; they too are pictures of courage. I thought of the August 6, 2011 tragedy that had ripped at my heart: those men also snapshots of audacity. The SEALs on board that downed helo had all stood there in those fin prints. I felt very small, as the prophet Isaiah in the Scriptures when he responded, "And who am I?" No. I could not stand there. I would not stand in such high caliber footsteps of courage. I knew that clearly; I was out of my element.

For you and me, all of those men, like Danny Dietz, never rang that dreaded bell of surrender. They stood there on that grinder so that someday, somewhere in the world in a place most of us have never been nor seen, with bravery beyond comprehension, they would stand, once again refusing to "ring a bell" of surrender: courage enacted, justice exacted.

No indeed, I could not muster up the courage to stand where courage had stood.

Medallion Moment

Life can sometimes deliver more challenge than reward, obstacles than opportunities. However, no matter what happens in life, like Danny Dietz we have to draw down deep from within and stand in whatever gap to which we are called. For some, like myself, it is their faith, passages of Scripture that reflect the truth that nothing can overcome us. Some draw strength from the lives of people, like Navy SEALs, who have blazed paths, lived well, or offered a helping hand. While for others, their courage is deepened by the words of a hymn, an anthem, or a story they shall never forget.

Since having the blessed time with this family, my courage has been deepened by a haunting phrase that both Cindy and Dan Sr. have shared with me. The phrase is not just about their son, but about all fallen warriors. "If they can endure what they endured, then what I am experiencing or about to experience—is nothing."

So true. Whatever life gives, whatever obstacle is hurled our way, we must keep things in perspective. If they can do that, then I can do this. Therefore, resolved, I will march on through my life. And yet this march we continue, whatever that march may be, will ultimately cost us something. And that cost may be high.

Courage to do the right thing, to make a stand, to embark upon your mission, to do whatever courage is calling—will come with a high price tag. With that thought, I return to the forefathers, the signers of the Declaration of Independence. According to Professor David Barton, many of the signers suffered great hardship during the Revolutionary War. Here are a few documented facts. Two of them were wounded in battle. Seventeen lost their homes and property. Several of the signers fled their homes just in time to elude capture. One signer had two of his three sons held as prisoners while the wife of another was held prisoner, resulting in her premature death. The son of another signer was killed in the war. [12] The stories continue, but I believe you see the pattern. Courage will always cost you something. I would purport that the very fear of the potential cost is the very thing that may paralyze a person from embarking on that to which they know is right or to that which they are called.

After all, fear paralyzes. Courage will never be the absence of fear. Courage is the refusal to adhere to the binds of fear. I cannot help but think of General George

Washington and his troops at Valley Forge. One time I had the privilege of sitting in a lecture by Hillsdale College professor Dr. Burton Folsom, Jr. on the topic of Washington at Valley Forge. Dr. Folsom shared that during that long and bitterly cold winter, the Continental Army lost eleven men a day to starvation, exposure, and disease. By springtime over a third of the men were dead all due to causes of the environment. Following such a devastating winter, Washington commanded his men to advance against the British.

As the British left Philadelphia toward New York, the Continental Army, what was left of it, challenged the British and beat them. In spite of their circumstances, in spite of the consequences, Washington and his men refused to be paralyzed by fear. According to the Hillsdale professor, upon being asked how they, the Continental Army, beat the British, history has recorded that a soldier said, "They were just firing bullets, we survived Valley Forge!" Ironically, conquering fear sometimes comes through weathering the rough circumstances of life. We think to ourselves, *If I can do that, what is this in the face of that?* But overcoming fear that may paralyze our lives is easier said than done.

We have heard the phrase "faith like a child." Is it possible that sometimes we need to have the "courage of a child" to say, do, or act upon that which is right? Like never before, America is in desperate need of such kid-like bravery, defined by Danny Dietz and his fellow brothers. We need this bravery at a personal and local level. Potentially there are people in your life, in your town, waiting for you to courageously stand in the gap for them. To you it may take a large step of courage of a seemingly small size in light of other courageous acts. Whether it may seem gallant or grandiose to you, to the person for which you intercede courageously, it may seem dauntless.

We need this bravery, this courage at a national level. Such courage without restraint, demonstrated by Danny Dietz, is the same bedrock ideals on which this nation was built. Whether it be the pilgrims taking their first steps on Plymouth Rock, George Washington forging across the Delaware, or Dr. King refusing to quietly sit by and accept injustice, all acted upon a call to courage. These calls of courage, along with the call of many others, has built the ideals of this great nation. And today we bear the torch to answer our own calls to valor with a willingness to make the steps necessary that we may be found faithful.

_____

_____

_____

_____

Section Two

Humble Thyself and He Shall Lift You Up

My heroes have always been cowboys…Always in search of and one step in back of themselves and their slow-moving dreams."

—Willie Nelson, "My Heroes Have Always Been Cowboys"

Essay One: The Life of a Cowboy

There is nothing more quintessential then the American cowboy. Tall in his saddle, the American cowboy would survey the land with the squinted eyes of a bald eagle in search of wrong, of a potential predator or threat. With his peacemakers holstered at his side, a Stetson to shadow his leathered face from the sun, and western boots to weather the harsh terrain, the American cowboy is a classical, peculiar image of strength.

A cowboy often seems to be a walking paradox. A true cowboy wouldn't start a fight, but he never ran from one either. He may throw a punch at the drop of a hat, but the punch was thrown to defend the defenseless. He would protect the many, but often found himself alone in his thoughts at the end of the day. Waylon Jennings and Willie Nelson in their legendary song displayed the conflicting image of a cowboy when they sang the Ed Bruce lyrics, "them that know him may not like him and them that do may not understand him. He's not always right but he won't allow his pride to ever make you think he's right."[13] The image of the ultimate humble hero.

At the age of five, there was nothing more special to DJ than his cowboy boots. Cindy shared that one day out of the blue five-year-old DJ declared his choice of career. He wanted to be a cowboy! For him as well, a cowboy was the ultimate image of heroic strength. Everywhere he went he wore those cowboy boots. To match the boots, he had his version of the Stetson hat and, of course, no cowboy is complete without his pistol, his peacemaker.

One summer morning, young Danny informed his mother that he no longer cared to wear the tank top and shorts she had chosen for him.

"I was confused," Cindy shared. "DJ had always worn whatever clothes I laid out on his bed. When I asked him why he no longer wanted to wear his normal play clothes, he responded that cowboys didn't wear t-shirts and shorts."

DJ proceeded to walk over to his closet and point to a western shirt and blue jeans. According to him, that was the proper attire for a cowboy.

On one other occasion, Cindy refused to dress DJ in the long-sleeved shirt and blue jeans during the summer heat. Begrudgingly, DJ put on the tank top and shorts given to him by his mother. Cindy returned to the kitchen only moments later, hearing the kitchen screen door slam shut. She looked out the window into the back yard. There he stood, bound and determined to look like the high riding heroes he admired, wearing his yellow shorts and green tank top, complete with his cowboy boots and hat. What an image.

Far beyond the clothes, DJ would show himself to embrace the inner spirit of the American buckaroo. As a child, he was never one to brag and always quick to please. Even up to the age of nine, having never lost a martial arts battle, he never mentioned it. He also never mentioned that his gymnastics work as a kid brought Olympic scouts. He simply had no need to boast. These were the young makings of a different kind of cowboy.

At first glance, humility and cowboy heroics seem to be another paradox. Someone audacious enough to charge into a situation that may very well cost them their life would seem to have a certain sense of boldness, of flash. But for a cowboy, boldness in the corral, on horseback, in the saloon had everything to do—with action. Talk was cheap. A braggart would find themselves eventually embarrassed. Actions spoke louder then hot air. The feats accomplished spoke for themselves and demonstrated whatever needed demonstrating. It was true for cowboys of yesterday, and today it is true for a different strand of cowboy, the American Special Operation Forces.

Essay Two: Others Before Self

In life, everybody needs somebody. And for Jamie, Danny was that somebody. As adolescent friends who spent a lot of time together, Danny and Jamie had grown close. Jamie had grown to rely on him, sharing her difficult moments of life with him, seeking his advice or support. On one particular night, after being out of town for a few summer months, she found herself really needing to talk with her best friend. She picked up the phone and dialed. No answer. She called again, only to receive—no answer. She called again and again, attempting several times throughout the evening to reach him. Admittedly, she was irritated. Had he not promised her he would always be there? And tonight of all nights, when she really needed Danny, he wasn't there.

The next morning Jamie called again, finally reaching her friend. Upset, Jamie began to vent her frustration and futile efforts trying to reach him by phone. She recounted the number of times she had called. She had been in some trouble and explained how she needed someone strong and couldn't reach her best friend. She furthermore reminded him that he had always promised to be there, and she felt as though he had broken that promise. As she vented, Danny sat quietly, listening to every word in silence, and finally she demanded an explanation as to his whereabouts when she needed him most.

There was a brief moment of silence. Danny simply said, "I'm sorry I wasn't there for you, Jamie."

He answered her question as to where he was with the following answer: the little sister of a mutual friend, sick with a serious illness, had passed away. The young teenage boy had spent the night at the hospital with their friend, mourning the death of the sibling. He did not attempt to make Jamie feel guilty. He didn't chastise or condemn her for her earlier demanding statements.

Now Jamie sat silent. Many years later as she recollected that story she shared, "He taught me a lesson that day: others before self."

On one other occasion, Danny had given this lifelong friend Jamie an anklet bracelet with a charm of two small feet representing her favorite poem "Footprints in the Sand." The anklet, according to Danny, was to remind her of the writing, and when life was bad, God would carry her through. After giving her his gift, she and DJ went rock climbing. As they neared the top of a mountain, the anklet became snagged on a jagged rock. Jamie looked down just in time to see the anklet falling down the side of the mountain. Once they reached the mountain peak, Jamie was visibly upset over the lost anklet. Without a word, Danny scaled all the way back down the mountainside, located the broken anklet, and climbed the long distance back to the top. With only a smile, he handed her the prized possession. Others before self.

On a separate occasion, during BUD/S, Danny placed himself in potential harm for a dear friend. Miraculously evading inspections and spot room checks, Danny concealed two pet chinchillas to present to this special friend following BUD/S. One can only imagine the consequences had his plan been uncovered! To this day, a Navy SEAL instructor is still amazed at his feat, on behalf of a friend.

Service, placing others before self, even when hiding chinchillas, only comes from a humble, contrite spirit. It was this humble spirit that brought the admiration of his fellow SEAL teammates. A selfless man of equals, Danny qualified for a coveted spot in sniper school. Needless to say an amazing honor, Danny chose instead to attend communications school. Less sensational, Danny made his choice because of a greater need. Others before self.[14]

Essay Three: No Applause Needed

Most of us know the old joke about the humble award. We usually apply it to someone who, let's say, is not so humble. Remember it? "We'd give him/her the humble badge, but they'd wear it." Truly the humble need little applause for the acts of service they perform. The humble don't seek recognition. There is no bragging required on their part. The Navy SEAL ethos says it this way:

> I do not advertise the nature of my work, nor seek recognition for my actions.

One of my dear friends, who spent over twenty years with the SEAL teams, once said, "You know I went off to BUD/S thinking I was going 'to become a Navy SEAL, then I'll come back and show a few people.' But man, the exact opposite happened. I went through BUD/S, completed my training, and for me—that was enough. I didn't need to show anyone anything."

Along this journey of learning about Danny Dietz, several stories will stay with me forever. One of those stories took place after a brief stint at home. Dan Sr. took Danny to the airport to catch a commercial flight to begin his long journey back to his deployment to an unknown location. When they arrived at the airport and Danny began to check his luggage, he produced his requested military ID, clearly marking his membership in the United States Navy. Dan Sr. watched from the distance as one of the workers, who had served in another branch of the military, teased Danny about being in the United States Navy. Danny smiled, never saying a word about his membership in the elite United States Navy SEALs. "I said to myself," Dan Sr. told me, "'you fellas have no idea who you are talking with.' He disappeared through the sliding doors, and I thought, *What a stud.*" Danny did not need their applause.

For a real cowboy, there is no time, no patience for applause or a media blitz. They either have too much to do, they just simply do not care, or a combination of both. Navy SEALs are called the silent professionals for a reason. They do their job, and for the most part they have the ability to keep their mouths shut about their capability. Like Danny, they do not need books, media attention, movies, spotlight, or recognition. They signed up to be a warrior—if you will, a cowboy—to defend the flag, uphold freedom, and serve their team. They did not sign up to sign autographs. They continue to be the living evidence that debunks the myth that all good cowboys wear white.

It seems that after all Danny reached his childhood dream and was indeed a true American cowboy: the courage to do the right thing, the humility to never mention it. He clearly did "not advertise the nature of [his] work, nor seek recognition for [his] actions" as that beautiful SEAL ethos states. How unusual for someone, for an entire community, to be so good at something, to be placed in positions of such importance for a nation, to conduct tremendous actions on behalf of an entire nation, and simply need no recognition. That was Danny. As one childhood acquaintance shared with me, "Danny wouldn't want any of the recognition given to him."

Dan Sr. was right. Man, what a stud.

Essay Four: Humility Is a Jewel

As a Navy SEAL, humility has often been attributed to Danny Dietz. One teammate shared that with all of his accomplishments, Danny was humble, never bigheaded or trying to show someone up.[15] His actions would speak; his words would remain unspoken. In some circles of society, where name-dropping and bragging are the modes of operation, such humility almost seems surreal and unheard of. And yet, that was Danny. And that was not just Danny the Navy SEAL. No, that was just Danny, a true gem.

One of the most stirring stories about Danny Dietz concerns his kid brother Eric. Eric had been involved in a serious car accident that potentially could leave him paralyzed. On deployment, Danny received the news concerning Eric and immediately made a request to receive temporary leave. Upon arriving in the states after numerous straight hours of travel, Danny came busting into the Colorado Hospital Intensive Care unit. He sat down next to Eric and began talking directly into his ear. As visiting hours began to wind down, an ICU nurse informed Danny, who had not moved from the bedside, that he would have to leave.

Not flinching a muscle and not looking up from the Eric's bedside the Navy SEAL said, "Ma'am, I did not fly twenty-odd hours to sit in a waiting room."

Nothing else was said.

Over the next week, Danny would not leave his brother's side. Doctors informed the family that Eric, suffering from a spinal injury similar to actor Christopher Reeve, may not ever walk again. And still Danny would not leave Eric's side. Over and over again he kept leaning down to whisper into Eric's ear. After a week of speaking into his brother's ear, it was time for Danny to return to his deployment. To this day the family does not know what their SEAL son kept uttering into his kid brother's ear. Yet a week after Danny returned to the battlefront, against all odds and predictions, Eric walked out of the hospital. Whatever Danny had said worked.

In a society where so many seemingly compete for recognition and praise, Danny quietly whispered in his brother's ear, sat at the bedside of dying girl, and performed numerous other acts of quiet, humble service. Sun Tzu called the humble warrior who advances without "coveting fame" a jewel. The ancient Chinese military general turned philosopher wrote:

> *The general who advances without coveting fame* and retreats without fearing disgrace, *whose only thought is to protect his country and do good service* for his sovereign, *is the jewel of the kingdom.* (emphasis added)[16]

Is that not the warrior of which I write, of which you read? On the battlefield he would advance without need of fame with only the thought of his country and team. Off the battlefield he would help others struggling to advance without need of applause and with only the thought of their betterment.

Returning to the adolescent account of Danny rescuing the gifted anklet, Jamie explained her reasoning in sharing the story. "That took place on a mountain. He went down the mountain with such ease and grace to retrieve my broken anklet. I can't help but think of the fact that he also gave his life on a mountain."

It would seem that on one mountain he rescued a gem, and using the words of Sun Tzu, on the other mountains— he became one.

Essay Five: The Deathbed of Humility

It seems that most recently I have been spending a good deal of time reading about and even discussing a word that has crept into American culture: entitlement. Whether it is studies conducted on generations, the comments of national politicians, or overhearing a conversation in the airport in which someone feels something is due them, the acidic ideal of entitlement is seemingly seeping into every aspect of our culture. The antithesis of the humility of which I write is arrogance. The deathbed of such humility is entitlement. For entitlement roars in arrogance, "This I deserve." Humility says, "This I shall give." Entitlement says, "This is not my fault." Humility says, "This is of my own making; therefore, I will have to make my own way out."

Late in his adolescent years, Danny made some key decisions to focus his pathway to becoming a Navy SEAL. Because of previous adolescent troubles (discussed in chapter four), ranging from school truancy to run-ins with legal authorities and court appearances, Danny had fallen behind in high school. In order to enter the US Navy, he had to have a high school diploma. At the age of nineteen, making him the oldest kid in a new high school, Danny pushed to achieve three years of education into one. At first, the age difference seemed to bother him, but he humbly accepted responsibility and did what needed to be done in order to enter the military and follow his dream of becoming the best of the best. Again, humility owns the consequences of one's actions, while entitlement purges any and all responsibility.

As well, growing up in blue-collar settings, Danny would have witnessed Dan Sr. often working two or three jobs to keep the family fed and bills paid. Is there any doubt that here he learned that there were few things in life to which he was entitled? Those who work hard, who serve seldom feel entitled. Those who feel entitled seldom work hard, never serving anyone beyond themselves. Special operators, which Danny so greatly represented, have little sense of entitlement. They serve, they give, they ask for nothing in return—like the image of a cowboy riding off into the sunset on the back of some stallion with no praise needed, no bragging to be expected, only the reward of knowing hard work was accomplished and service was rendered. Is that not the image, the sort of leadership we so desperately thirst for in America today?

While entitlement is the deathbed of humility, Danny and these men teach us that humility can in turn deal a deathblow to entitlement. Entitlement is darkness. Humility is light. Entitlement offers no path to freedom found in giving to others. Humility takes the focus off self, off current circumstances, to serve others with no need of reward or recognition. These men, Danny and his beloved Navy SEALs who have been so celebrated by media and entertainment venues, are so much more than the tactics they use, their feats of physical strength, and amazing military endeavors. These men, these warriors offer us a glimpse into lives well lived. They offer us an image of leaders who have set aside that which was potentially "due them" in order to risk all, give all in service to team, in service to you and me.

For while courage, according to Churchill, is the first of human virtues, many a philosopher, thinker, and theologian would argue that humility is the foundational virtue. While courage is needed to actualize uprightness, Confucius maintained that humility was "the solid foundation of all the virtues."[17] Saint Augustine believed that humility was fundamental to religion. According to him, there was little actual virtue in a soul that lacked humility, only the appearance of virtue. [18]

In humility lies true service. Yet those who live only to have their needs met will likely find death to their soul and emptiness to their life. Moreover, those who live for themselves die by themselves. In direct contradiction to the darkness of entitlement, the Navy SEAL ethos, which articulates their motive and mode of operation for service, states:

> Brave men have fought and died building the proud tradition and feared reputation that I am bound to uphold. In the worst of conditions, the legacy of my teammates steadies my resolve and *silently* guides my every deed. (emphasis added)

This legacy that potentially steadies their resolve is one of steadfast courage, lived out in humble acts of service. This legacy is one of team before individual, country above all, and that no man shall ever be left behind. Such a legacy, left by Danny Dietz and others who have fallen, is living evidence that the humble never die; their actions live on in those who follow behind them. For truly the Scriptures are correct when they proclaim that those who humble themselves before their God will in due time be lifted up.

Medallion Moment

In the Old Testament, Proverbs 18:12 warns that before a downfall "the heart is haughty." That text continues, however, with the admonition that "humility comes before honor." Such humility, as defined by the preceding essays, blended with courage, is what so many so long for in America today. Yet I cannot help but ponder that so much of humility is simply controlled strength. Humility knows that with the power and the capability one has the wisdom to use that power in service, and the ability with consistent strength to allow actions to speak and words to remain unspoken. Seemingly, braggarts are the insecure and weak, while the humble are the confident and strong. Maybe those who talk big very well live very small lives. And maybe those whose actions are big, yet their talk of self is limited, live limitless lives of strength and confidence. Maybe. But for sure, while pride does come before a fall, the humble are honored. And within such honored humility we can find a bedrock principle: the service of others before self.

The arrogant will never serve anyone outside of self. They find only pleasure in the service of ego, the preservation of self. In complete contradiction to such self-oriented thinking is the Navy SEAL ethos maintaining that members of that coveted community will place "the welfare and security of others before my own." Often we find ourselves longing for a Danny Dietz persona to serve us in our business, faith, or political arenas. Maybe instead of longing for it, we must become that or demonstrate a life of others before self. In other words, instead of waiting to witness it in someone else—be that someone else. Simply put, others are waiting for us to give of ourselves.

And with such humble service it is true that much will be required from us, most likely with little praise or recognition. However, it is one thing to serve and give; it is another thing to serve and give and do so without that need for recognition or praise. We must be willing to decrease "us" in the moment. We have to be willing to do whatever it is that needs to be done, for the simple sake of doing the right thing. Is that not what real leadership ought to be about? Is that not what we want in those we elect, follow, and place our trust and belief? After all, so much can be accomplished with little recognition or credit.

This form of humility was what John Winthrop spoke of in his famed "A Model of Christian Character" sermon.[19] In voyage to the New World, Winthrop addressed future colonists in 1630, admonishing them to claim the words of the Old Testament prophet Micah in doing "justly, to love mercy, and walk humbly with our God."[20] Such humble service to God and to each other would, in the opinion of Winthrop, become part of the fabric that would, quoting the New Testament book of Matthew, set America as "a city shining on a hill."[21] America shines, for many reasons, and among those reasons is the character of her people. Former President George W. Bush said it a different way, that "Ultimately, the success of a nation, depends upon the character of its people."[22] Danny Dietz has left us such an example.

I referred to Danny, quoting Sun Tzu, as a jewel. A jewel, a beautiful jewel, stands out. Among a million rocks, one can spot such a shiny precious stone. Among a million pieces of fake costume charms, a jeweler can spot the real diamond. And in society today, among all the screaming voices yearning for attention, isn't it easy to spot the contrite? In a world that continually says, "Look at me, look at me!" is it not easy to spot the humble, the civil? Maybe it's because actions will always be louder than words. Maybe it is their indifference to recognition. Whatever the reason, surely the humble are truly a jewel. Those like Danny Dietz who perform great acts with great humility make America a great nation.

Danny's life and legacy heeds to us a warning: that entitlement is the deathbed of humility. He humbly took responsibility for is actions and what he needed to accomplish to make right—the wrong. Entitlement, with her tentacles of destruction, is quickly weaving herself through our culture, attempting to choke life and liberty from society. We cannot, we must not replace the very character that has made America a beacon for so many years with an ideal that simply takes from those around it. We must purpose to lift the value of humility, the bright jewel of humble service, so that we can shed light into the darkness of the culture of self. And when we do this, others surely will follow, and together we will live out the words of that Proverb passage, "Humility comes before honor," leaving a legacy for all times.

_____

_____

_____

_____

Section Three

Signs of Genius

There are no great limits to growth because there are no limits of human intelligence, imagination, and wonder.

—Ronald Reagan

Essay One: Intelligence as a Virtue

Recently, around my home I have exhaustively used a phrase. Anytime I do something slightly strange, like a weird cartoony voice or something awkward, such as trip over my own two feet, I look at my wife and say, "That's a sign of genius, right there." Everything imperfect, impractical, slight, or greatly weird or a mistake I have made has all become "signs of genius." Such phrasing does bring a rather positive, albeit ridiculous, spin to any given moment.

Danny Dietz had signs of genius. The only difference is his were real. At the age of six, DJ scored several points above genius level on proficiency tests.

"I made a pledge to myself that day," Dan Sr. told me, "that he was not going to waste his intelligence."

Danny Dietz was a certified, born genius. As a kid, he was enrolled in the talented and gifted programs where he intellectually thrived. And yet for Danny, his intellect was not just book smarts. Book smarts is one thing; intelligence is something else altogether.

Albert Einstein said that intelligence, "is not knowledge but imagination." He claimed he wasn't smarter; he just stayed with problems longer. Really, Albert Einstein was not smarter? I must admit I struggled when first reading his words. After all, his last name has almost become synonymous with the word smart. We've all heard the phrase, "They're no Einstein," or after a bad decision someone sarcastically yells, "Way to go, Einstein!" Yet according to the genius, he wasn't really a genius; he just "stayed with a problem longer." Hmm…

That sent me to the virtual pages of the online dictionaries, searching for a definition of intelligence. Here is what I found according to Merriam-Webster:

> Intelligence a (1): the ability to learn or understand or to deal with new or trying situations: reason; *also*: the skilled use of reason (2): the ability to apply knowledge to manipulate one's environment or to think abstractly as measured by objective criteria (as tests)[23]

When you break that definition down, you actually return to Einstein's words, that he just "stuck with a problem longer!" Intelligence is the ability to learn or understand or deal with trying situations. It is the ability to apply reason or knowledge to manipulate one's environment. I believe the Navy SEAL ethos says it better:

We expect innovation. The lives of my teammates and the success of our mission depend on me—my technical skill, tactical proficiency, and attention to detail. My training is never complete.

This is where we begin to see intelligence as a virtue. Others depend upon the applied knowledge, the ability of their teammate to learn, understand, or deal with trying situations. And that sort of attention to detail matters, and it matters a lot. When it comes to Danny Dietz, a retired Navy SEAL with over twenty years in the NSW community said it best. Asking to remain nameless, he stated:

He was the consummate SEAL. That kid was so smart, so smart. In my time, I never met a guy [a SEAL] as smart as Danny.

Essay Two: Death of the Box

Who created the box? How many times have we heard the phrase, "Oh, that's so out of the box?" What box? Where did the box come from? Is there some little living being, a troll, some guy with a beard running the Matrix that creates the boxes? After all, what determines what a box is or the boundaries of the proverbial box? Are you getting my drift?

I can answer my rather rhetorical and ridiculous questions with a paraphrased quotation I once heard. The only box created is the one we create for ourselves. Intelligence, applying knowledge, destroys any box that may attempt to contain it. One Navy SEAL commenting on Danny relented that if the plan made could not be executed, Danny would find a different way. And that way was typically better to begin with.[24]

No box, creative thinking demands that the walls of any box, of the status quo, even at times "what makes sense," be destroyed. Creative thinking examines all potential solutions, obstacles, outcomes, possibilities, and so forth. This no-box thinking sets odds aside, even if for just a minute, and examines what could be. Such analytical thinking takes whatever situation it is found in and finds a way to do what needs to be done. For a special operator this sort of processing is crucial. We need to look no farther than their ability to conceal as an example of such creative thinking.

It is no huge secret that Navy SEALs are known for their expertise at being—secret(ive). Their conceal training, knowing how to blend into their surroundings, is unmatched and near miraculous. Their ability to take their extensive training, apply their own intelligence, and move in and out of insurgent strongholds without the knowledge of the enemy is the stuff of legends. It gives Hollywood the cold sweats. It makes ordinary people shake their heads in disbelief. They simply make camouflage, ghillie suites, and stealth movement into a form of art. During this part of training, Danny Dietz excelled. Again, there was no box.

"He laughed with me when he came home from his training," Dan Sr. shared. "He said, 'Dad, they couldn't find me. I was concealed, and they searched and searched, but they could not find me. But when they found me, they still worked me over.'" Only later, as Cindy spoke with individuals from the SEAL community, did the rest of the story emerge. Rumor has it that Danny not only evaded capture during a particular exercise, but he also ultimately captured one of the training instructors! Whether or not it is related, this particular training exercise was removed for a short period following Danny's escapade.

Even as a kid, he displayed his love for such imagination, for such creative thinking. "I was a caretaker at a cemetery," Dan Sr. shared. "That was one of the jobs I held. And not all that long ago a friend I worked with, a mechanic that worked there at the cemetery keeping the machinery working, reminded me of something. I would sometimes take Danny with me to work. At that point Danny wanted to grow up and be a Ninja. My friend said he was always amazed at Danny's ability to sneak around. He loved thinking through how to be stealth, sneaking around, and not getting caught. In fact, my buddy and I would stand there chatting, and out of nowhere Danny would appear, attempting to spook us."

Maybe, just maybe, that is why Sun Tzu in "Art of War," said:

> It is only the enlightened ruler and the wise general who will use the *highest intelligence* of the army for the purposes of spying, and thereby they achieve great results. (Emphasis added)[25]

In essence, a wise military leader sends out the smart ones for spying and reconnaissance. The smart ones never see a box; they only seek creative solutions.

Essay Three: My Training Is Never Complete, the Love of Learning

At age six, DJ began reading the dictionary. You read that correctly. At age six he began reading the dictionary. It gets worse, I mean better. Often he would pull down the Encyclopedia Britannica, sounding out large words, and read about topics most of us learn about much later in life. It goes one step further. At around the same age, he began reading medical books. I was floored too.

Clearly, he had a reading comprehension level that was well beyond his years. And clearly DJ loved to learn. But I will never forget the interview when suddenly Dan and Cindy blurted out the fact that Danny read Dan Sr.'s medical books. I thought the Skype connection we were using via the Internet had broken up for a moment.

"I'm sorry," I said, "Did you say he read medical books?"

They laughed at my shock. "He would read my medical books," Dan Sr. continued sharing.

"Wait a minute, folks." My shock was a little more than obvious. "You're telling me that he read medical books, like the ones needed to become a doctor?"

"Yeah, I was going to community college at the time in hopes of becoming a physician's assistant," Dan Dietz shared, "putting to use my past work as a navy corpsman. He would pull my medical books down and skim through them."

I again felt the need to clarify with Dan Sr. and Cindy at what age DJ was reading dictionaries, encyclopedias, and his medical books. Dan responded in the affirmative that it was, "about six or seven years of age." I'm not sure my mouth closed for the rest of the conversation.

So how did reading the dictionary, encyclopedias, and medical books start for a child at the age of six? According to both parents, Dan Sr. had shared with young DJ a story from his own military days.

"We had this injured guy who came into the medical ward. He was considered a genius. And everyday that ole boy would read the dictionary. He would read encyclopedias. So I shared that story with Danny." And as a young boy, barely in school, Danny Dietz decided he wanted to be just like that man.

"I always wanted the kids learning," Cindy Dietz-Marsh added. "I always had them somewhere before DJ entered school. We would go to museums, the park, the zoo, and other places."

At a very young age, DJ was given the love of learning. There are a lot of gifts we can give our children; I have to believe that the gift of learning is on the top of the list. This sent me back to an Internet search. How many times have I used the phrase a lifelong learner? Yet what defines that? I smacked the words, "What is a lifelong learner?" into a Google search engine box. Immediately I was nailed with numerous articles on "steps to becoming." I pushed away from Google and re-read a quote from Dan Sr. about the bop bag. Remember the bop bag, a punching bag for four-year-olds?

Dan Sr. revealed the following:

> It is something else that he spent so many hours on that thing. But Jeremy let me tell you what was even more amazing: the moves he was performing. Jeremy, they were my moves! Moves as an

instructor that I taught! I would be working with a student, and I would look over and see these little eyes peering around the corner watching me. One day I was watching him on that bop bag and realized that at age four he had been memorizing all the moves I was doing and teaching. And there was as a four-year-old, mimicking to perfection those moves.

Wait a minute. He observed. He learned. He practiced. And then he repeated those steps. After re-reading that quotation, I no longer needed my Google search. And yet it doesn't end there.

Moving into his teenage years, Danny would often busy himself building obstacle courses, extensive obstacle courses. He would start with a large tire, moving it up a hill and down the hill, then back up again. Following his tire exercise he would have an object, like a chair, in place for fifty standing free jumps. The next part of his course might be a high number of push-ups, followed by scaling the side of his childhood home. From there he would emerge on top of the garage roof performing, as a friend shared, "ninja moves." In essence, with his eye on the goal of being a SEAL, it seemed that Danny felt his training was never complete. He would build one course, observe, learn, and build another course. See a pattern? And this sort of training, building obstacle courses to overcome, is as much mental as it is physical. Maybe that is why he later set the obstacle course record during SEAL training in Coronado, California.

Essay Four: It All Leads to Something

Do you ever have one of those moments where you briefly look around at your life circumstances and wonder, *Where the heck is all of this going? Where am I or where is this moment going to end up?* Maybe you're driving to work, headed to the grocery store, or dropping off the kids somewhere and you find yourself daydreaming, wondering about the direction of your life journey. Maybe it's just me, but I think a lot of people have these wonderings. Someone once told me that life was a journey. And along the journey are certain mile markers, certain situations that lead from one to another. And in that journey each step, whether it is easy or difficult, will ultimately lead you to the destiny in which God has for you.

Look at Danny Dietz and his unique story. Genius level intelligence matched with a love of learning and what seemed to be an amazing ability to absorb knowledge gave the Navy SEAL program their ideal warrior. So with that, as I wrote the preceding essays on intelligence, I felt as though there was a piece missing. It felt as though there was an additional essay needed. I kept asking the same questions: What else do we draw from this? What else do we learn? What else can we garner from Danny, from other heroes of this and other wars? Do we need to study harder, read more, train our minds or try to be a knowledge sponge? I knew there was something missing; I just could not put my finger on it.

So I kept returning to the essays, combing over my words. I reviewed in my mind the different stories. I looked back at the interviews. I searched through my interview notes. And finally I turned to my wife, Christina, and asked her the same questions, laying out the case of this section. Her response brought my heart to a standstill:

> Sometimes you think not everything is a lesson, and you don't realize that they were lessons until you get to the very end. I wonder if Danny realized, in his final moments, that everything he had learned, all of his intelligence, his whole life had led to that point.

Got it.

He wasn't reading the dictionary to become a Navy SEAL. Right? He didn't desire to follow the military guy in Dan Sr.'s story so he could become a special operator. No, all the stories in these essays were just stories of an all-American kid who loved to learn, who loved to train, and who eventually desired to be the best of the best. Yet along the way, even during his hardest moments of adolescence, Danny Dietz's training was never complete. He was picking up life lessons, learning what he needed to learn, and taking each step to the next step that would lead him to his destiny.

Before leaving to enter BUD/S, a friend shared with Danny her concern about the inherent dangers of his chosen profession. "He looked at me and said, 'Everyone has a calling, mine is to be a Navy SEAL.'" And that was that.

Medallion Moment

The founder of the University of Virginia, Thomas Jefferson, wrote that, "The qualifications for self-government in society are not innate. They are the result of habit and long training." On one other occasion, the forefather who only wanted to be known for his university founding once wrote, "A honest heart being the first blessing, a knowing head is the second."[26] Jefferson understood the charge for education in the preservation of liberty. This inventor, author, statesman, author of the Declaration of Independence, first secretary of state, and third president of these United States valued intelligence and its application to life. Without the virtue of applied intelligence, democracy, freedom ceases to exist. However, someone cannot apply that which they do not have.

Socrates once said, "The only true wisdom is in knowing you know nothing."[27] Have you ever met the person that seemingly has no point of ignorance? In other words, they have all the answers to everything. They simply have no point in which they are clueless. There is a problem with that line of arrogance. Einstein said he wasn't smarter; he just stayed with a problem longer. Einstein did not have all the answers. He had a point of ignorance.

The Navy SEAL program is not looking for people with all the answers; they want people with a point of ignorance. Do you see the pattern? Learning requires the previous virtue humility. The willingness to admit we do not know. After all, how can a person apply knowledge if they never believe they have need of any? But with intelligence, knowledge, and wisdom comes the needed strength to view life differently, not from the status quo or the ordinary.

It is acceptance of a box that is a deathblow to creative thinking. When we accept the stale phrases of, "We have always done it that way" or "We have never done it that way" as truth, we in essence lie to ourselves, consenting that "playing it safe" is merely just accepting the inevitable. Whether these box-oriented thinking phrases are spoken internally by us or by others to us, we accept the norms of a situation, leaving it unchanged in exchange for their approval. Whichever way the cards are dealt, we bring Reagan's words to life: the only box created is one we create for ourselves.

Danny spent his life destroying boxes. How? He would observe. He would learn. He would practice. Repeat. Nothing complicated about that, except doing it. His learning and his training both physically and mentally were never complete. Lifelong learners, whatever the steps may be, observe, learn, practice, and then repeat. They do not get comfortable with the knowledge and abilities they hold; they seek ways to enhance their strengths, other skills, new wisdom that will better enhance their life and work. Though they may not purpose to destroy boxes, they just do by the very way in which they live and practice life. For while many marvel at the abilities of special operators, we ought to mimic the mindset they have, that Danny had, that learning, that training is never complete.

So where can we learn? Obviously from sources of knowledge such as people and writings. We can learn from Danny. Mentors, classroom settings, family members, and those we respect offer great lessons. We can even learn from those who never learn, marking that we shall never follow their path. Everyday life offers a unique and difficult obstacle-training course for knowledge application.

Let's face it: life happens. Sometimes we fail to take a breath, allowing ourselves to get caught up in the storm of the moment, whatever that moment may be, without any focus and sometimes without hope. There is a good chance, a very good chance that every lesson along the pathway of life has prepared you to handle what you are facing or will inevitably face. Maybe the lesson was a previous life moment. Maybe the lesson was in the book. Whatever the case, if you have been a student of life, understanding your training is never complete, you are ready for the moment that lies in front of you. Chuck Swindoll had it right when he wrote, "We are all faced with a series of great opportunities brilliantly disguised as impossible situations."[28]

And so it is today as a nation. Without becoming too political, America is clearly at a crossroads, a deciding point. In our two hundred plus years of history, we have seen economies rise and fall, battles lost and won, faced challenges that redefined the word "insurmountable," and created a history rich as a nation that always has a tomorrow. The question that lies before us today is not one of what we will do, but how we will do it. Will we, quoting Jefferson, apply our "habit and long training" to that which we face today?[29] Will we value intelligence and education in facing "great opportunities" that are so "brilliantly disguised as impossible situations?" I believe we will. I believe we must.

_____

_____

_____

_____

Section Four

Integrity the Hard Way

Making their way, the only way they know how.
That's just a little bit more, than the law will allow.

—Waylon Jennings, *Dukes of Hazard*

Essay One: Wisdom for the Future

Greek biographer and essayist Plutarch once opined that:

> To make no mistakes is not in the power of man;
> but from their errors and mistakes the wise and
> good learn wisdom for the future.[30]

As we just discussed, life is a great instructor, if only we have the humility by which to learn from it. How often have we met those who garner little wisdom for the future? They continually fall into the same holes, trip over the same habits, deny education and wisdom from others, all the while garnering the same bad results. And from that mindset they garner no wisdom.

Like many heroes, Danny had more than a few opportunities to learn "wisdom for the future." Before a life-changing moment that steered him to his dream of becoming a Navy SEAL, he was kicked out of two high schools, ran away from home more than a few times, evaded the police, and wound up being processed in the court system.

Often we place our heroes at such a high level of admiration and respect that we forget something so simple and beautiful: they are human. While true heroes deserve such admiration and respect, we often forget that they tripped, they fell, they made decisions that earned them their virtue, their character. In essence, those we label heroes often made some mistakes along the way. For many warriors-turned-heroes they seemingly opted to learn and develop their character—the hard way. This brings me to one of my favorite stories concerning Danny.

As a teenager Danny Dietz, future American hero, future Navy SEAL, found himself running from the local police. At this time in his life, Danny had enacted his above-average talent in arts to graffiti tag old buildings. While we are not sure if the local authorities happened to be on patrol and found Danny and a group of boys or were called to the scene, a chase ensued, and the police pursued Danny on foot. He lost them, as the boy could flat out run anyone. Once Danny lost the police, they did not find him again. The local authorities searched for him to no avail. Where had the kid gone? Little did they know as they searched for him, that he was right above them. The future Navy SEAL had hoisted himself up the side of an eighteen-wheeler, laying flat on the roof of the trailer, hiding in plain view from the authorities. This is where the story becomes interesting.

On this particular evening, in an area not far from the semi-truck that concealed Danny, was a police helicopter. Hearing of the situation, the patrol helicopter offered to lend a helping hand, or better yet a huge spot light to assist in the pursuit effort. The helicopter came swooping down, its massive light shining its beam into every corner and facet of the area—no Danny. Now if you have ever watched a television show in which a fugitive was pursued by a police helicopter shining its bright light, you know how difficult it is to remain at large. However, on this night the helicopter could not locate the future Navy SEAL. Danny would later recount that as the helicopter arrived on the scene, he scaled back down the side of the massive eighteen wheeler, crawled underneath the trailer, hoisted himself up under the truck, and concealed himself in order to evade the authorities—once again.

I cannot be the only person who finds this story slightly amazing. Maybe I should not admit this, but as a law-abiding citizen, I was impressed by this account. Why? It reveals so much about Danny and his future as a Navy SEAL. It is not so much that Danny Dietz made some "bad" decisions; it is what those decisions symbolized and what he in finality did with those decisions that beg our attention. First, he had a mischievous spirit (Dan Sr. calls it "ornery"). Boy genius was in search of adventure and risk. After all, everyone makes bad decisions. Sometimes we make bad decisions because of poor information, the wrong acquaintances, or ego, to name a few. At other times the bad decisions we make are simply our strengths, our strong points in life pushing the wrong way, running amuck, or looking for an outlet. As a teenager Danny had abilities that were beyond normal. He concealed himself and moved with such stealth that local authorities could not detect him. His adventurous and daring spirit was screaming to emerge. At the time these were strengths and talents pointing in the wrong direction.

Secondly, while bad decisions have consequences, the hopeful outcome is the garnering of "wisdom for the future." Danny would take his human strength, abilities to run fast, stealth movements, and the ability to conceal himself and use them for good in service to his country. From his past he clearly learned. After all, there are individuals who have the same brushes with the law, make the same bad decisions, who continually live in that pattern their entire life. These individuals never learn from their past failures. I often tell my business clients that for them failure is not the problem; failure to learn from the failure can be devastating.

For Danny, his adolescent years became a school of hard knocks to train for the future. As he went through his initial screenings and trainings to become a Navy SEAL, he would, from time-to-time, write thoughts and favorite quotations in a notebook. Within that notebook we find an entry that notes Danny's strengths are pushing in the right direction, that he has garnered wisdom for the future. We will never know which parts of this statement potentially meant more to Danny than others. However, I could not help but underline certain lines in light of this essay. Not long after entering BUD/S Danny copied by hand Wanda Hope Carter's "To Achieve Your Dreams, Remember Your ABCs."[31]

Avoid negative sources, people, places, things, and habits.

Believe in yourself.

Consider things from every angle.

Don't give up and don't give in. Don't give up what you want most, for what you want at the moment.

Enjoy your life today, yesterday is gone, and tomorrow may never come.

Family and friends can be hidden treasure. Seek them and enjoy their riches.

Give more than you planned to give.

Hang on to your dreams.

Ignore those who try to discourage you.

Just do it! You can't build a reputation on what you're going to do.

Keep on trying. No matter how hard it seems, it will get easier.

Love yourself first and foremost. Learn from your past.

Make it happen. Do what you can, with what you have, where you are. Make decisions today that you will feel good about tomorrow.

Never lie, cheat, or steal. Always strike a fair deal. Not everything that is faced can be changed, but nothing can be changed until it is faced.

Open your eyes, and see things as they really are.

Perfect practice makes perfect.

Quitters never win, and winners never quit.

Read, study, and learn everything important in life. We are what we repeatedly do.

Stop procrastinating. Start from where you are; it is the only place you can.

Take control of your destiny.

Understand yourself in order to better understand others.

Visualize it. Want it more than anything. Victory is not about never failing. Victory is starting again if you have a slip or relapse.

Winning is not everything. Get satisfaction from doing. No Whining!

Xccellerate your efforts.

You are unique. Nothing can replace you.

Zero in on your target, and go for it!

Essay Two: Taking Responsibility for the Wrongs

Integrity can be tough. First off, we have to desire the ideals of integrity. Secondly, we have to be willing to accept the outcomes that are often the result of having integrity. In the pursuit of integrity, we know there will be moments that doing the right thing will be more difficult, more dangerous, or cost us something greater than people without integrity would pay. Integrity generally comes with a high cost. If there were no cost, if it were always easy, would not everyone do the right thing all the time? As well, is that not why we sometimes may temporarily lack the virtue as we weigh that the cost of the outcome is too high?

Moreover, maybe for some the most difficult piece of the virtue owns up to the moments when we lacked integrity. People who seek to do the right thing often find themselves apologizing because they did the wrong thing. Integrity requires us, demands of us to take personal responsibility for our actions. A person on the pursuit of honesty longs to do the right thing, and there is an internal clash when humanity kicks in and potentially wrong choices are made at a moment of lax judgment. Truthful people take personal responsibility for their actions. They simply hold themselves accountable.

In order to share an amazing moment of an American hero righting his wrong, we first have to look at a few of Danny's ill steps. On one spring afternoon, he decided to borrow his grandmother's car. The problem was that Danny's grandmother did not know he had "borrowed" the car. There he was, cruising down the road at a top speed with two friends joining him for the escapade. One friend sat in the front seat and the other in the back seat. I have little doubt that they were probably cheering Danny on as he decided to play his own version of the Dukes of Hazard. "Making [his] way, the only way [he] knew how..."[32] at an unknown rate of speed, Danny earned the dubious distinction of going airborne in that Ford Taurus, placing it precisely in the middle of a river. One passenger ended up with a broken nose; the other with a broken leg. This would not be the only incident involving an automobile.

One other time, Dan and Cindy were called to a courthouse in another county to pick up their son who had been involved in a physical altercation. The story unfolded like this: Danny was driving along with his girlfriend and younger brother as passengers when he became involved in a verbal altercation with two men in another car. At some point seventeen-year-old Dietz got out of his car to face the two grown men. These men, twelve to fourteen years older than Danny, assumed that between the two of them they could easily handle the teenage boy. They assumed wrong. In fact their assumption earned them a visit to the hospital. After they were humiliated by the teenager, the grown men decided to press charges against the minor. The presiding judge threw the case out, saying that if anyone should press charges, it should be the parents of the minor Danny Dietz. This would not be the only time Danny appeared in a courtroom. Due to other indiscretions, Danny and his parents would appear in court three additional times. The relationship between Danny and his parents became tense.

As hostility at home grew between Danny and his parents; arguments and verbal exchanges escalated. One evening following one of these altercations, Danny was sent to his bedroom. Once there, he proceeded to open the window, scale down the wall, and run into the darkness of the night.

"All I saw," recounted Dan Sr., "was the back of Danny running down the street. And boy, could he run."

That night, Dan and Cindy found themselves scouring the city deep into the morning hours looking for their son. On one other occasion, the verbal argument became so heated between father and son it nearly came to physical blows.

"I remember," Dan said, "that I wanted to give up. But this lady [Cindy] looked me in the eye with those steely eyes like Danny's and said, 'You never give up on a child.' And she was right."

It was tough. Danny was skipping school, running away from home, associating with the wrong crowd, and making choices that broke the heart of his parents.

As I listened to these stories, I kept thinking about the superhero movies we watch in the local theater. There is always a moment of tension, of dissidence in which the hero seems down and out or has made choices that frustrate the viewer. We are sitting there with our oversized barrels of popcorn thinking to ourselves, *Come on, what are you doing? Don't you see what is happening? Don't you see the potential?*

As Danny's parents recalled the past, I experienced that same feeling that I have experienced many times watching a hero-based movie. I wanted to fast forward through these stories and jump to the place of redemption. I wanted to get to the place in the story where Danny pulls it altogether and becomes this amazing Navy SEAL that many still speak of today. Yet we could not. These stories, and others, were part of Danny Dietz. And in his moment of redemption came some actions that still bring tears to this author's eyes.

Not long after entering some of the final phases of his Navy SEAL training, Danny called his father. They discussed what Danny could discuss about his new life as a Navy SEAL in training. Dan Sr. caught Danny up on all the news on the home front. Then there was a moment of silence followed by a tone of voice that signaled a boy becoming a man.

"He told me," Dan Sr. recalled with tears in his eyes, "that he now understood some of the lessons I tried to teach him. And that he was so very sorry for all the things he had done."

Never again would Dan Sr. refer to his son by his childhood nickname DJ. After becoming a Navy SEAL, for the rest of his life Dan Sr. would call him Danny. As according to the father, "He had become a man."

In becoming a man, Danny took ownership of past indiscretions. Not long after earning his trident and becoming a Navy SEAL, Danny returned to his hometown of Littleton, Colorado, to visit with family. A few days into his visit he began talking with his mother about the events of just a few years earlier. They talked about the tough times, his decisions as a teenager, and even some of the fallout from those decisions. Mom and son talked about how well he was doing in the military and that he had fulfilled his dream of being a Navy SEAL. Suddenly Danny looked at Cindy with remorse in his eyes and said:

> Mom, I am so sorry. I am so ashamed for what I put you through during my teenage years. I wasted a lot of time. I could have been here [Navy SEAL] a lot sooner. I wasted your time. I am so sorry. I never meant to hurt you. I love you.

Redemption.

Essay Three: Wrong Armor

Danny Dietz was not that good at being a "bad boy." At heart he was a warrior, not a gangster. According to Cindy, at age thirteen he began wanting to dress different, in oversized shirts and blue jeans. It seems that Danny was a warrior in gangster clothing. This reminds me of the Old Testament story of a shepherd boy waiting to be a king. As a shepherd David knew how to protect his flock of sheep. After all, the guy had killed both a lion and a bear with the jawbone of a dead animal. He too had the heart of the warrior.

Before he was given the nod to become a king, the famous story of David and Goliath took place. If you remember the story, David had been sent to check on his brothers who were at war with his country's arch nemesis, the Philistines. While visiting with his brothers, David overhears the bellowing calls of Goliath, the giant champion warrior. Amid criticism and probably doubtful laughter, the short and ruddy David begs for the opportunity to face off against the giant. The military leader King Saul knew that David was the underdog. Saul insisted that David wear his own armor into the one-on-one battle with Goliath.

Have you ever seen someone wearing a tuxedo or dress suit that was two sizes too large? The jacket shoulder pads hang off to the sides. The pant cuffs drag the ground. They simply look as though the circus called and they have been volunteered for clown duty. I can only imagine that David, who was much shorter than the tall and gallant Saul, looked similar. David walked around for a bit and then politely said, "I don't think this will work for me." (Unless it was a strategy in hopes of making Goliath laugh himself to death.) David removes the armor, grabs his slingshot, five smooth stones, and heads toward the battlefield. The rest, as they say, is history. David understood that he was a warrior trapped in the clothing—the armor—of someone else.

Danny Dietz was a warrior trapped in the clothing of someone else—a gangster. Along the journey of adolescence there were glimmers that Danny was not in the right suit of armor. That was certainly confirmed when he "borrowed" Grandma's Ford Taurus and mimicked the "Dukes of Hazarded" into the middle of a river. Upon escaping the sinking car, Danny noticed that his injured friends were trapped in the car. He did not run from the scene in self-preservation, as a gangster only living for himself, and protect his own skin. With water rushing into the windows of the Ford that was sinking like a rock, Danny dove back into the water, not once but twice, to pull his friends from the sinking car to safety. A warrior in wrong clothing.

Remember the story of Danny getting out of his car facing two men much older than himself? While it is amazing and actually humorous that he whipped those two men, there was a reason he even engaged them. While we are not sure how the entire altercation began, we do know that the men were making careless comments toward Danny's girlfriend. In addition, his younger brother was in the car witnessing the vulgar exchange. He did not fight without cause, according to his account; he fought to protect the both of them and to defend the girl's honor. A warrior in wrong clothing.

Just like the future King David, Danny Dietz had a moment, a brilliant moment in which he realized, maybe was reminded, that he was wearing the wrong suit, the wrong outfit, the wrong armor. Finding himself on a path bound for juvenile detention or worse, the once little boy who tested above genius was in grave trouble. Sitting in the judge's chambers, Dan Sr. and Cindy were desperate for direction, help, answers, or suggestions. As they sat talking to a judge, their third time appearing before him, he offered a potential solution for Danny: a juvenile boot camp. Upon hearing about the boot camp for troubled juveniles, Danny was ecstatic. He could not wait to attend. This would be his closest yet to feeling like he was living his dream: being a Navy SEAL.

Once at the boot camp, the future silent professional excelled. The physical and mental demands along with the rigorous schedule and discipline were the perfect recipe for Danny. It was in that camp that Danny made his life-changing decisions, experienced a type of re-awakening, and refocused his strengths, those unique abilities, and his genius-level thinking toward his ultimate goal. In other words, like David the shepherd boy, Danny proclaimed that "this current gangster dress and mindset" would not work for him. He changed his armor. Now was his time.

Essay Four: The Strength of a Nation

My grandfather was a World War II hero. He used to tell us riveting stories from his deployment in Germany. He told stories ranging from a harrowing voyage across the

English Channel, stunning stories of going door to door in search of Nazis following the air force invasions, and of his conversion to Christianity in a foxhole. (I remember him saying, "We never knew what was going to be on the other side of that door.") As I recall some of those stories, I have no doubt my grandfather left part of himself in those European villages. He also left part of himself with me.

Growing up with my grandpa sitting in the warm West Virginia sun drinking Coca-Cola and eating peanut butter and crackers, he would often quote Scriptures to me. The one that still stands out in my mind today is "a good name is rather to be chosen than great riches" from the wise King Solomon.[33] As a kid I listened to that phrase, not completely believing it. However, as an adult I have met people and read accounts of others and their wealth. Often their names have been tarnished. My grandfather was right. However, I do not believe he was speaking of simply having a good reputation. After all, it was Thomas Paine who told us that, "Reputation is what men and women think of us; character is what God and angels know of us."[34] No, my grandfather was trying to teach me to always do the right thing because your name, what people know of your character, matters, and it matters a lot.

Danny Dietz understood this. According to reports, as an adult he was more interested in doing the right thing rather than polishing his reputation. On one trip home to Littleton, Colorado, Navy SEAL Danny Dietz went to visit a few buddies from his high school days. At some point a conversation ensued that would seemingly lead Danny back down the paths of his adolescent ways. Navy SEAL Danny Dietz became furious at the suggestion of the indiscretion. A verbal altercation broke out among the old friends, and Danny stormed off, refusing to take part. As mentioned in the first essay, he had truly garnered wisdom for the future. He had changed his direction, and he refused to go back.

Business philosopher, coach, and leadership expert Jim Rohn once stated:

> Character isn't something you were born with and can't change, like your fingerprints. It's something you weren't born with and must take responsibility for forming.[35]

A good name and becoming a person of integrity is a choice. As a grateful nation, we thank God that Danny Dietz made the right choice. As a man, as a Navy SEAL, Danny would embody the words of the SEAL ethos:

> Uncompromising integrity is my standard. My character and honor are steadfast. My word is my bond.

At the ceremony posthumously awarding Danny the Navy Cross, a fellow SEAL teammate in tribute labeled him "a man of integrity."[36] In another interview by the Denver Post, a close friend and fellow Navy SEAL characterized Danny as "a man of integrity who excelled at everything and always went out of his way to help others."[37]

Such integrity, common to all special operators, is the foundation upon which our nation was built. Our forefathers believed that in the moment of fire, uprightness would trump self-preservation that good would win out as the choice and that wrong and any evil foe would be vanquished. After all, it was our first American president George Washington, a warrior in his own right who at many levels set the moral tone of our country, who said, "I hope I shall possess firmness and virtue enough to maintain what I consider the most enviable of all titles, the character of an honest man."[38]

My grandfather left a legacy. He embodied integrity, character, and wisdom and taught a young boy by his life and words that nothing was more valuable than these qualities. Likewise, Danny Dietz came to grips with his own destiny, turned his life around, and channeled his energy into a positive force for good and for this great country. After all, we are a nation of second chances. We are the people who believe in starting again.

Medallion Moment

For some it may seem strange, even awkward to speak of Danny Dietz's past indiscretions under the heading of integrity. Nevertheless, there is one thing that we humans all have in common—a past. We all have a past lined with milestones of goodness, trail markers of good intentions and even the litter of the not so good. We have made decisions that sometimes are less than stellar. Decisions that, in the words of Willie Nelson, leave regret "just a memory written on my brow."[39] But as Willie Nelson concedes in the same song, "There is nothing I can do about it now." For the problem will never lie in the past.

The problem is when we fail to learn from our past. In learning from the past we can impact what we are doing in the present. In essence, what did we learn from our past decisions, the consequences, the results? And now, what decisions are being made today that will equal different results tomorrow? We simply cannot allow ourselves to be a prisoner to our past.

In a joint message to Congress just one month before signing the Emancipation Proclamation, President Abraham Lincoln proclaimed:

> The dogmas of the quiet past, are inadequate to the stormy present. The occasion is piled high with difficulty, and we must rise with the occasion. As our case is new, so we must think anew and act anew.[40]

So it is the same, on a much smaller scale, for each of us. We can listen to the dogmas of the quiet past, or we can rise to the present and change our future. Ultimately, just like Danny discovered, the power is in our hands. And part of that power to change the future is not living in the past, yet making mends where mends can be made.

Redemption is painful and is the process of recovery, which only comes when one takes ownership of his or her decisions. We have to own our mistakes, poor choices, and the potential consequences and fallout. Danny never made an excuse for any of his past actions. He simply owned them and with great courage said three words that some people never have the courage to utter: I am sorry.

Integrity demanded of Danny Dietz, and it demands of us, not to blame anyone else for our action. Integrity earned implores us to own our choices, to admit our wrongs, and to seek forgiveness. Even as I pen these words I can think of more than a few folks to which I owe the words, "I am sorry." That is most likely true for many of us. Two questions demand of us an answer: Will we have the character, the integrity to say those three powerful words? And then will we have the courage of character to move on beyond the past?

Danny Dietz demonstrates to us that both of those questions can be answered in the strong affirmative. He made his mends. He made his difference. As an adolescent Danny ran from the authorities and was starting toward a future of trouble. As a Navy SEAL he ran into trouble as an authority on combat. As an adolescent he used his ability to hide, to keep from getting caught. As a Navy SEAL he hid, concealed in order to help catch Islamic terrorists. As an adolescent he graffiti tagged buildings with art; as a Navy SEAL he used his art to design T-shirts for his BUD/S Class 232.

While every strength we have been given has the potential for good or bad, every person, on many occasions, will also have to make a cognitive choice concerning their strengths. As we stare down that proverbial fork in our path, we will once again be forced into a situation that demands of us an answer: Will I work on behalf of good or on behalf of self?

Bordering on the line of becoming cliché, I cannot help but think of the most stirring moment in the comic book movie series *Spider Man.* In a moment of recollection, Peter Parker recalls a conversation he held with his deceased uncle. Under immense pressure, standing at such a fork in the road of decision, desiring revenge at many levels, Peter Parker is humbled into the understanding of doing good when he recalls his uncle's words, "With great power comes great responsibility." That comic book hero narrative represents the decisions made by Danny Dietz and numerous other warriors and civilians alike. And it is the decision of integrity to do the right thing that continues to bring America to greatness.

So everyday is our moment to make that right choice. With the Navy SEAL ethos, pledging that, "Uncompromising integrity is my standard. My character and honor are steadfast. My word is my bond," it is clear everyday that these fine warriors recommit their being, their soul to such living, making it almost commonplace for them. So let it be commonplace for us. Let this virtue of learning from our past, of owning our decisions and simply doing the right thing become the driving force of our decision making. And then let us have such nerve to take the words of the Navy SEAL ethos and quietly proclaim them as our own:

> Uncompromising integrity [shall be our] standard.
> [Our] character and honor are steadfast.
> [Our] word is [our] bond.

PHOTOS

Pictured at four weeks old, DJ would be walking only a brief eight months later.

A cowboy at heart, at the age of three DJ already loved his cowboy boots and hat.

DJ at age two demonstrates one of his
many moves in the martial arts.

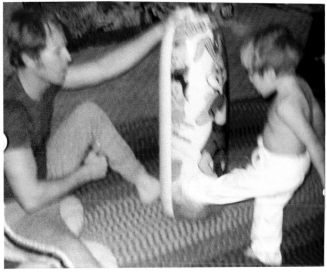

At age four DJ practices beating up his bop bag.

DJ pictured during his Kindergarten year of school. Already, he had begun to show signs of genius level intelligence.

DJ pictured with mother and father during his graduation from the court-ordered boot camp. This experience would change his life forever.

Danny pictured shaking the hand of "The Old Bullfrog" before the pinning of the Navy SEAL Trident.

One of few pictures with Danny wearing the Navy SEAL Trident. Danny would never allow Cindy his mother to take a picture of him in uniform wearing the Trident.

Taken the Spring of 2005, Danny is pictured with fellow Navy SEAL Shane Patton. Shane Patton was aboard the Chinook CH47 that was sent to extract Danny and his teammates.

Armed to the teeth, Danny Dietz prepares for final mission as a United States Navy SEAL.

An avid animal lover, Danny with his beloved
dogs Nox, a Tosa Inu and Charlie Murphy (after
the Charlie platoon) a French Bulldog.

Danny pictured with younger sister Tiffany and brother Eric.

The Dietz family during Christmas 2004.

Of the ten Navy SEALs pictured here, only one (Marcus Luttrell) would survive the June 28, 2005 mission.

Resting in his bunk in Afghanistan, Danny had a picture taken for family. In the background we see his weapons, a witness to the severity of war.

Danny being carried to his final resting place by his brother Eric, Uncle Ghassan and teammates.

The picture above is Danny Dietz boarding a helicopter. Following the June 28, 2005 mission, the family labeled this photo, "Danny Walking to Heaven."

Max Robert Coyle of Williamsburg, VA, at
the age of five salutes an American hero.

Section Five

Rock Solid Steadfastness

Be sure you put your feet in the right place, then stand firm.

—President Abraham Lincoln

Essay One: Resolved—A Common Man with an Uncommon Desire to Succeed

We Americans admire steadfastness. As a nation, the deep-seated belief in persistence is entrenched deep into our psyche. We simply rebuff the idea of giving up. It is who we are. After all, it was American inventor Thomas Edison who said, "I haven't failed. I've identified ten thousand ways this doesn't work."[41] We marvel at those, maybe with odds stacked against them, who seemingly ignore the idea that they were "supposed" to quit. We have "Americanized" the words of famed British Prime Minister Winston Churchill: "Never, never, in nothing great or small, large or petty, never give in except to convictions of honour and good sense. Never yield to force; never yield to the apparently overwhelming might of the enemy."[42] We cling to such words as we watch re-runs of movies with characters like Rudy or Rocky Balboa. No matter how hard we get hit, no matter who has tried to dissuade or push us back, we marvel in the notion that no matter what, we will never quit. Are we not the nation of the Alamo?

This steadfastness, this persistence, this mindset is what separates men from boys, success from the mundane, and heroes from mere mortals. What Teddy Roosevelt told us many decades ago applies today:

> We need the iron qualities that go with true manhood. We need the positive virtues of resolution, of courage, of indomitable will, of power to do without shrinking the rough work that must always be done.[43]

A brief study of history quickly teaches one that the quotation above came from a man who earned the words he spoke. As a young boy, Roosevelt was of poor health, weakly, and frail. Through sheer iron-will and the challenging of his father, Roosevelt would confound doctors by defeating illness and working himself into a robust man. A sickly boy would exercise and work his way into a man who literally gave a campaign speech after taking a bullet to the chest. For Roosevelt it started as a boy. The same is true for many a Navy SEAL, including Danny.

It appears that Danny's resolute, steadfast spirit began at birth. "Once that boy got his mind set on something," Dan Sr. shared, "there was little anyone could do to dissuade him."

At the age of two, Danny's resolute spirit came shining through when the small family of three entered a bike-a-thon to help raise money for a local charity. Danny was offered the normal opportunity to ride in the seat attached to the back of his father's bike. The little boy refused that idea, insisting that he would peddle his red tricycle in the two-mile race. Even after Cindy's explanation that two miles was a long distance and that he would become tired and his legs may even hurt, he continued to hold forward his determination to peddle his tricycle. In addition, Danny made it clear that not only did he want to ride his tricycle in the two-mile event, he was resolved to win the charitable ride! When he was informed by Cindy that there were no winners in a bike-a-thon, his stubborn determination would not be swayed. He would peddle his own tricycle, and he would win, even if there were no winners. Now it is one thing for a toddler to proclaim intentions of a huge action; it's another altogether to follow through!

Danny followed through.

As the bike-a-thon began, dawning an orange construction flag on the back of the tricycle, the two-year-old began pushing the peddles of the red tricycle with all of his might. Both Cindy and Dan Sr. were convinced that halfway through DJ would become tired and simply want to ride on the back of his father's bicycle in his attached seat.

"Just about the time that I would start to think that maybe DJ's legs were hurting," Cindy shared, "he would turn around and look over his shoulder at Dan and I and yell, 'Hurry up, Mom,' or 'Come on, Mom. Peddle faster.'"

He completed the two-mile-ride peddling as fast and hard as he could. And following the "race", well into the evening time, DJ never once complained.

A picture of tenacity.

Essay Two: Hard Work

Apathy will seldom beget the virtue of steadfast, unless an individual is steadfast about being apathetic. Laziness will never result in steadfastness, unless a person is steadfast about avoiding work. According to the Collins English Dictionary, the very definition for "steadfast" calls for hard work:

> Steadfast: 1. fix in intensity or direction; steady. 2. Unwavering or determined in purpose, loyalty.[44]

Fixed in intensity or direction with little unwavering, our determined purpose does not simply happen. People who are steadfast, who are marked with a determination so firm, are typically marked with the value of hard work. What did Roosevelt tell us in essay one? That rough and hard work were iron qualities, as it is not effortless to be resolved.

Men without the drive to do the rough work cannot hack the endurance of a special operations community who believes, "The only easy day was yesterday." Numerous articles and books have detailed the strenuous work of becoming a Navy SEAL. Men much more qualified than me have written in-depth about Indoc, Hell Week, and the different phases of BUD/S training. However, as I perused through the different books I own about Navy SEAL training, I was once again amazed that there is training for their training. The men spend five weeks in indoctrination course (Indoc) learning how to conduct themselves in the upcoming phase one of BUD/S training. The SEAL candidates begin the grueling non-stop physical training piece, learn how to conduct themselves around the pool, how to handle their small inflatable boats in the Pacific Ocean waves, and begin internalizing the warrior ethos. The percentages of men who drop out during the entire Indoc and BUD/S phases seem to vary from book to book between 80 and 90 percent. Only 10 to 20 percent of those who begin the grueling process will actually complete the training path, earning their trident and becoming a Navy SEAL. I think it is fair to purport that qualifying to become the best of the best requires more than just a good attitude. In fact, it requires more than what most men can afford to give. To say it takes hard work is quite the understatement.

Danny Dietz thrived in training to become a SEAL. Even though he was briefly set back for a medical reason, Danny worked extremely hard during his days in Indoc and the different phases of BUD/S. His sheer grit, determination, and hard work earned him the respect of his peers and instructors. According to the records obtained from Coronado, with only forty-six men left in SEAL Class 232, Danny was ranked by his peers as number three and by all six instructors in the top five for his performance. In addition, Danny Dietz would set the course time record for the infamous obstacle course (O-Course). With its high and short walls, the hanging and towering cargo net, and barbed wire trenches, the O-Course is a struggle for any athlete. Yet Danny, if you remember from an earlier chapter, had been training for quite some time.

As an adolescent, Danny's physical training was non-stop. Every morning he was up and out for his early run. In addition to his basic weights training—the previously mentioned self-made obstacle courses with oversized tires, high knees, and scaling the side of his boyhood home—were by any measure extreme. He would push and push, running faster, farther, doing all that he could and then some to remain strong and build strength. "He would treat his body like a temple," Cindy commented concerning her son's physical fitness routine.

Steadfastness requires and comes with the value of hard work. Roosevelt's quotation from essay one is clear: such qualities require the power to not shrink from the hard work. One SEAL teammate, on Danny's memorial page, recounted a story concerning a land navigation course. In the required course time, Danny was unable to make it to a mandatory final point. Drenched in sweat with exhaustion, Danny refused the customary ride in the truck back to camp offered by instructors to those who had not completed the course. Danny walked the long distance, arriving back at camp hours after everyone else had returned[45]. He would not shrink from the necessary work that may be difficult. He just would not quit.

Essay Three: There is Resolve, Then There is Resolve. Never Quit

There are some people who seem to have a little bit more of a crusading push inside of them. It could be labeled drive, but that does not quite cover it. It may even be labeled as perseverance, but that too falls short. These are the people that nothing seems to stop them. They get knocked down by life, by circumstances, by others, and they always get back up again and again. The only words I believe that come close to accurately labeling this form of steadfastness are those words from Teddy Roosevelt that have framed so much of this section: indomitable will. In doing a quick dictionary check of the word "indomitable," the following sentence comes glaring off the computer screen:

> Incapable of being overcome, subdued, or vanquished; unconquerable.[46]

A human spirit so determined that it cannot be squashed, will not retreat, and will not under any circumstance surrender or give up. This form of resolve is simply unstoppable.

Welcome to the inner makings of a Navy SEAL. They do not quit. They will not stop. They simply keep pushing until they cannot push any farther, and then when it seems they may be out for the count, down on the mat, they stand up and push with a strength and inner will that appears almost inhuman. That is resolve, beyond resolve. That is indomitable will.

However, there seem to be few in America who would have us believe that this attitude of being unconquerable is something of our past. It is a harshness that worked in Teddy Roosevelt's day but not so much in the modern America. Today, somehow, we have come to a new turning point in our country where everyone is a winner and every action is equal. It is prevalent thinking that a first attempt or simply trying to solve the problem once is enough. However, there is nothing further from the truth. The biggest problem with those failed arguments can be summed up in two words: Danny Dietz. His resolute spirit of which I am about to share is symbolic of each and every United States Navy SEAL.

As a child, after spending hours on his previously mentioned "punching bag for a four-year-old" bop bag, he would then challenge his father to a round of sparring. Dan Sr. would sit on the floor with his hands up, defending himself from the fierce onslaught of his son. Then Dan Sr. would reach out from behind his hands and tap Danny on top of the head. The boy would not allow his father to get the best of him. Danny would turn around, walk away from his father, and return to the bop bag and practice all of his moves again. After significant practice, he would return to his father, enter his starting position for another round, and begin sparring again. When his father would once again get the best of him, Danny would return to his bop bag for more practice, repeating the process. This scenario went on for quite some time as Danny was growing up. One day, in the middle of this common routine, Dan Dietz realized something, "DJ was hitting harder."

This spirit of refusing to be subdued manifested itself in the boy learning to ride his bike. Danny was convinced that he could learn to ride his bike in only one day. At the age of three, the future special operator was bound and determined that the training wheels were to be removed from his yellow bike and that he would conquer this scientific ideal of balance. Once Dan Sr. and he were in the field across the street from their home, the future Navy SEAL would not allow gravity to get the best of him. He would not quit in the effort to master his bicycle.

"Oh, it was painful to watch," Dan Sr. shared. "I would guide him along and then give him a push, and off he would go, peddling as fast as he could, and then down he would go. And he wouldn't quit. He would jump back up and want to do it all over again."

Full of refusal to surrender, the three-year-old continually pedaled a short distance, falling again and again into the grass. As the day wore on, DJ became stronger at pedaling. With stronger pedaling came harder crashes. Numerous times, the three-year-old boy would flip over his handlebars.

"I would just stand there," Dan Sr. shared with a wince on his face, "and just cringe, thinking that surely this time he would be ready to quit for the day. But nope, not DJ. He would jump back up, grab the bike from the ground, and yell, 'Again, Daddy, again! Again, Daddy, again!' We would do it again, he would flip over the handlebars, jump up, and yell, 'Again, Daddy, again!'"

By sunset DJ had reached his goal and mastered the art of riding his bicycle in one day.

Another example of a boy with indomitable will is DJ and the pumpkin race. At the age of six, Cindy entered DJ in the annual school pumpkin race.

"He loved to race, and he was so fast," Cindy shared, "so I entered him in this fall race. At the time DJ's sister, Tiffany, was a toddler, and I was expecting our third child, Eric."

It was an unseasonably warm fall day when DJ, Cindy, and baby sister Tiffany showed up for the all-school challenge pumpkin race. DJ had already made clear his intentions to win. When the students lined up for the start of the race, DJ looked over at his mother with a grin that said, "I got this." Many years later, that same grin, caught on video uploaded to YouTube, would be seen by BUD/S instructors in Coronado. When the signal was given to begin the race, DJ shot out of the starting line with no one able to match his speed. Though he was running well ahead of everyone else, he never slowed his pace. He never looked over his shoulder. He was going to easily win, yet he did not give any of his competitors even one second or one inch by which to gain on him.

"When he crossed the finish line as the clear winner, we were all cheering," Cindy shared. "Suddenly I see DJ fall to the ground, and he doesn't get back up. I came out of the sidelines dragging Tiffany beside me. When I got to his side, I realized he had passed out from the heat. He never did handle heat well, even later as a SEAL."

Driven by his indomitable will, Danny had purposed to not only win, but win with little challenge near him, whatever the cost.

He lived his whole life that way. Most special operators do. The world was first introduced to the iron will of Danny Dietz in the aforementioned YouTube video of BUD/S Class 232. The video is a small documentary, an insight to the strenuous path of becoming a Navy SEAL. Several days and numerous physical exercise repetitions into the week, we see Danny Dietz. Countless hours of physical activity, miles of running, numerous times in and out of the cold waters of the Pacific ocean, and Danny Dietz is spotted in the video, standing in his element, thriving on the adversity of no sleep and physical training beyond human comprehension. By the time we see Danny, most likely numerous men have already rang the bell on the grinder, signifying they could no longer handle the abuse of the training. In the video for a very brief second, Danny looks at the camera. In that second he displays a lifetime of virtue. For on his face is neither a frown of concentration nor a look of despair. No, Danny Dietz is smiling, actually smirking. It was a grin that appeared to be taunting, "Is that all you got? I so got this."

It would be sometime later during BUD/S that Danny would set the previously mentioned obstacle course record time. By the way, unbeknown to his instructors, Danny set this long-lasting obstacle course record with a broken ankle.

Indomitable will.

Essay Four: The Mountain

I have pictured Danny, in my mind, at least a thousand times. The harder the Taliban hit with their mix of AK-47 fire and rocket-propelled grenades, the more resolute Danny became. I continually picture this young twenty-five-year-old Navy SEAL from Littleton, Colorado, refusing to give up. As the darkness of the War on Terror surrounded him and his teammates, the more resolute he became. I just keep picturing him. I have reserved the section "Nine and Never out of the Fight" to cover more about the happenings of June 28, 2005, the final mission of Danny Dietz. However, I would be remiss to write of steadfastness and not mention in part what took place in

Afghanistan. The one account we have of Operation Red Wings, along with all the other theories of what happened that day and even other reports, point to the same thing: Danny Dietz (along with his teammates) just would not quit. The after-action report found on a website honoring Lt. Michael Murphy states that when the battle had finished, there were thirty-five Taliban dead.

At one point in the fierce gunfight, according to Marcus Luttrell's *Lone Survivor* account, Danny was once again hit by enemy fire:

> He dropped his rifle and slumped to the ground. I reached down to grab him and drag him closer to the rock face, but he managed to clamber to his feet, trying to tell me he was okay even though he'd been shot four times.[47]

According to the account, in spite of his numerous injuries, Danny Dietz stayed in the battle. As if here were once more stating as he did when learning to ride that bicycle, "Again, again." Danny would take a bullet, a shrapnel hit, be knocked to the ground, but on the ground he would not remain. "Again, again." In those final moments of his life, the "common man with an uncommon desire to succeed" became the living incarnation of the Navy SEAL ethos:

> I will never quit. I persevere and thrive on adversity. My Nation expects me to be physically harder and mentally stronger than my enemies. If knocked down, I will get back up, every time. I will draw on every remaining ounce of strength to protect my teammates and to accomplish our mission. I am never out of the fight.

Marcus Luttrell, the lone survivor of the final mission of Danny Dietz, referred to Danny as a "caged lion." I have a feeling that the moment Danny spotted the enemy coming over the mountaintop, he resolved to do whatever he had to do. In no way would he leave the field of battle. In no way would he surrender. And when the gunfire began, Danny knew the odds against him, but he had faced odds before. Even as he was hit by shrapnel, by bullets, nothing was going to knock him down. Nothing.

"Again, again."

Medallion Moment

Courage is the will to confront. Steadfastness is the will to remain. For courage may bring you to a moment that others may flee, a steadfast will demands that you remain in that moment without passing thought of surrender. Courage gives the will to fight; steadfastness gives the will to remain in the fight. Those who are resolute spend little time peering around at the obstacles that encompass them. They will not accept no for an answer, nor succumb to the idea of total failure. If they count the entire cost of their actions, they know, they believe that whatever end goal lies ahead will be worth the price paid. They accept as truth the words of Napoleon Bonaparte when he said, "The truest wisdom is a resolute determination."[48]

No matter how great the odds seemingly are, those with such emotional and moral stamina continually push or find ways around that which is blocking their path. To paraphrase a famous quotation, the greatest determination of a person is what it takes to knock them down. Danny Dietz and all special operators have a sheer determination, an iron-gut resolution that nothing, nothing, nothing can stop them, let alone overcome. They are the embodiment of Sir Winston Churchill's words, "Never, never, never quit."

While it may be easier to quit, a determination of not quitting requires hard work. I am reminded of a childhood tale, the Aesop fable of the ant and a grasshopper who held different opinions concerning the value of work. During the months of summer, the ant worked hard to store up the needed food to survive winter. The grasshopper would spend the entire summer in a life of luxury, singing and relaxing. As the fable unfolds, the merry grasshopper inquires of the ant as to why he will not simply stop working, listen to his song, and relax. In some accounts the ant responds to the taunt of the grasshopper with a warning of the oncoming winter season; in other accounts the ant ignores the grasshopper and continues carrying an ear of corn, much heavier than the ant, above his head. We know the rest of the story. Winter arrives, and the ant's hard work pays off, and he and his colony survive. The grasshopper's song ceases as he begs of the ant to find survival.

Those who fear hard work, who run from its inevitable ways, will never be or become steadfast. When idleness takes up residence in a person, as it did with the grasshopper, it will ultimately destroy them; in the process lethargy can potentially drain others around that person in numerous ways, albeit spiritually, emotionally, financially, or physically. Those who are steadfast are those who work to achieve. Those who flee from hard work, the "rough work," will be the first to give up in retreat when life gets tough and obstacles emerge. After all, the old phrase, "When the going gets tough, the tough get going," plays out in an even larger extent when it comes to hard work. If a person flees from tough work, then it is easy to believe they will flee from life when it too becomes tough.

Fleeing is never an option for those who are unyielding. For the resolute, there is something too final, too terminal and so conclusive to the word conquered. Looking through history, we seemingly never hear from that which was conquered. Refusing to be conquered has a feeling of cheating death, of stealing back time from eternity. The steadfast, with an indomitable will much like Danny Dietz, smirk at such a notion of finality.

And in that smirk, a self-satisfying facial expression, a message is being communicated: "I am better than this. I am bigger than this." This sort of smirk at the possibility of thorough defeat takes a moral aptitude beyond comprehension. To step above the jaws of defeat and strongly resolve, "Courage brought me here, and here I shall remain." This indomitable will is steadfastness extreme.

For me it is an issue of my Christian faith, an anchoring of my soul that proclaims with the Psalmist, "Whom shall I fear?"[49] For others it may be a different anchoring of the heart. But make no mistake about it, there will be numerous moments when vanquish will be lurking around the corner. And it will be that very refusal to succumb, the will to press on, the determination to choose faith rather than fear and strength rather than weakness that will set apart those of the unconquerable spirit from those of the feeble.

I am reminded of the words of Roman poet Virgil when he wrote, "His resolution is unshaken; tears, though shed, avail not."[50] Tears may fall, yet over those tears the unwavering will not stumble.

In the Scriptures, King David, the warrior's warrior, wrote in Psalm 61:

> Here my cry, O God; listen to my prayer. From the ends of the earth I call to you, I call as my *heart grows faint;* lead me to the rock that is higher than I. For you have been my refuge, a strong tower against the foe.[51] (emphasis added)

At some point the great warrior was seemingly at a point of surrender, his "heart had grown faint." Courage had brought him to a moment in which his own indomitable will was beginning to weaken. Yet through his God he remained diligent, purposed, and steady. In our moments the victory or defeat is not determined by whether we become weary, tired, frustrated, or out of options. Our victory or defeat is determined in those moments by the actions we take. And in those moments what we do will ultimately define who we are.

After all, we will all grow faint. Life will take it out of us. Circumstances will emerge and surround us. And when it does, may we return to the words of Winston Churchill:

> When we look back on all the perils through which have passed and at the mighty foes that we have laid low and all the dark and deadly designs that we have frustrated, why should we fear for our future? We have come safely through the worst.[52]

_____

_____

_____

_____

Section Six

Loyalty: No Greater Love Hath He

Well done, thy good and faithful servant.

—Matthew 25:23

Essay One: Loyalty Defined

Every Memorial Day, observed the last Monday of every May, draws the attention of millions of Americans to local and national memorials, monuments, and national cemeteries as a nation remembers those who have given the ultimate sacrifice for freedom. One special ceremony will be recognized for its honor to the unknown, the nameless warrior. The national media will take you to this hallowed and most honored place—the Tomb of the Unknown Soldier, Arlington National Cemetery. On this day, along with Veteran's Day, the commander-in-chief or some other appointed dignitary will place, in military ceremony, a wreathe at this tomb. And while this ceremony will mark a national remembrance, a continuous ceremony offering the final picture of loyalty takes place at that tomb every minute of every hour of every day with a twenty-one-gun salute.

The twenty-one-gun salute is the most supreme honor given by the United States military. This traditional symbol of respect comes in many different forms and venues marked by type of weapon used, number of rifle party members, etc. The sentinels that guard the Tomb of the Unknown Soldier offer their own form of this highest honor. The precisely dressed honor guard crosses the plaza on the black mat in twenty-one exact and precise steps. Upon crossing from one side to the next, the guard will turn and face the Tomb of the Unknown for exactly twenty-one seconds. This is known as the silent salute. The military sentinel then turns again, pausing for twenty-one additional seconds before crossing the plaza in twenty-one steps to repeat the process. The weapon, the traditional M14 attached with a chrome bayonet, is carried on the shoulder away from the tomb as a warning and deterrence to any outside intrusion upon the tomb. Fully aware of their surroundings, these guards are more than just ceremonious toy soldiers. As they protect the Tomb of the Unknown, they will thwart intrusions from the public into the area the general public is not allowed. In addition, in a deep tone of voice, the tomb sentinel has been known on occasion to step off the mat, break silence, and remind the general public to remain standing or silent in honor of the fallen.

They stand at attention, giving the constant symbolic twenty-one-gun salute, guarding that tomb three hundred and sixty-five days a year. Through hurricane, blistering heat, or bitter cold they stand in honor, keeping watchful eye against intrusion, never abandoning the post.

Loyalty.

The tomb sentinels of Arlington National Cemetery are a constant reminder of the definition given by one dictionary of the word loyalty: "a devoted attachment."[53] There is nothing that stands in the way of the sentinel's mission. Nothing interferes with the objective of protecting that tomb; nothing impinges the loyalty they have to that post—not the elements, not others, nor hour the of the day—to that Unknown Soldier who has been laid to rest.

When you look back through this book, it is possible to take most of the stories and fit them into the idea of loyalty. Many stories of Danny and his loyalty as a Navy SEAL have emerged. One such story involved a fellow teammate who had overlooked some details. And for these guys, it has to be all about the details. Instead of letting it go, Danny took care of the overlooked portions and then talked with his military brother. He chose to be loyal to his teammate instead of choosing to let him wind up in huge trouble.[54] He was loyal to his community outside of the US Navy, volunteering to work with children in the local elementary school, designing, creating, painting, and building an entire production set for their annual school play. And those who know him best will usually say, "But that was Danny." And it was.

Once again, this virtue—loyalty—cannot be taught during BUD/S or in the process of becoming a Navy SEAL. It is something these boys bring with them from childhood. For the Dietz family, loyalty to family was a bedrock belief.

"We wanted him to learn to protect his sister and his younger brother," Cindy Dietz shared. However, the future Navy SEAL did not always see it that way. When Dan and Cindy first brought home their second born, Tiffany, from the hospital, Danny made his feelings quite clear about the new sibling.

"Take her back," the two-year-old demanded of his mother. She responded that such a possibility was not possible. Danny was not happy with the new baby. Some days later Cindy heard a crash come from the bedroom that held Tiffany's bassinet. Cindy ran down the hall into the room to see young Danny, her DJ, standing over the crashed cradle. Amazingly, the baby had not fallen out of her basket. Quickly, Cindy deduced that her son had pushed over the bassinet. Standing there with an expressionless face, he simply reacted with the cool response, "Take her back."

Within this story we may see the beginnings of the loyalty of Danny Dietz. It would be at this moment of his young life, giving Cindy the scare of her young life, that he would begin the journey of learning to protect his sister. From that point, Cindy and Dan were convinced that Danny understood the virtue of protecting the weaker, of being loyal to his family.

As a boy, Danny Dietz began to learn through his family and his church the value of such faithfulness. One of the most moving stories following Danny's death, comes from his Sunday school teacher. In a Denver Post article dated July 15, 2005, the Reverend Larry Herrera said he, "remembered praying with [Danny] Dietz in his Sunday school class when the future commando was a young boy. [We] talked about the lessons of Jesus, how he died so that others could live."

In the printed story, Herrera states the following:

I don't know if that seed was planted in Danny that day, but I know he had an example who died on the cross. There is no greater love than to lay down your life for your friends.[55]

Essay Two: The Protector, the Shield

It's a logical step. If you are loyal to someone or something, you will protect it. While there are different levels of loyalty (spouse, sporting team, country, military unit, and so forth), this form of allegiance is an unyielding attachment, a devotion to that which one is most loyal. And that sort of virtue (along with the others) requires a certain level of commitment. Whatever or whoever you find yourself attached to with devotion, you will defend at all costs. (Even individuals who are attached with devotion to only themselves, loyal only to their self-preservation, protect themselves.) The SEAL ethos states:

> I humbly serve as a guardian to my fellow Americans always ready to defend those who are unable to defend themselves.

Danny's Navy Cross citation gives a picture of his desire to protect when it states:

> Demonstrating exceptional resolve and fully understanding the gravity of the situation and his responsibility to his teammates, Petty Officer Dietz fought valiantly against the numerically superior and positionally advantaged enemy force. *Remaining behind* in a hailstorm of enemy fire, Petty Officer Dietz was wounded by enemy

fire. Despite his injuries, he bravely fought on, valiantly *defending his teammates* and himself in a harrowing gunfight, until he was mortally wounded. By his undaunted courage in the face of heavy enemy fire, and *absolute devotion to his teammates*, Petty Officer Dietz will long be remembered for the role he played in the Global War on Terrorism. (emphasis added)

Defending those who could not defend themselves, being a guardian loyal to those around him, as previously stated, began as a child longing to be a cowboy and a ninja. It became a natural piece of young Danny to protect those needing a shield. In battle, a warrior would use a shield to intercept attacks or to protect himself. Whether it is a small animal, friends, or his younger siblings, Danny was always ready to be that shield.

One day as we sat talking about her son, Cindy explained that "DJ loved animals." Growing up, Danny Dietz was used to having animals around. (One such animal was a huge dog that young DJ named Killer of Mooses. Later this large dog would break his chain, escaping the yard to never be seen again. DJ would never forget that dog.) Over DJ's lifetime they had dogs, chickens, cats, and other strays. When it came to animals of any shape and size, DJ loved them. And that which he loved, like all of us, he protected.

On one occasion, around age eight or nine, while standing in her kitchen, Cindy turned around to see DJ flanked by his younger siblings and holding a basket with a towel covering the top. Without saying a word, he handed the basket up to his mother. Cindy looked down at the three siblings with a confused look. She looked back at the basket now in her hands and slowly lifted the towel to peak inside. Before she could see inside, loud hissing sounds arose from the basket. Startled, she screamed with fear, as the basket crashed to the floor. Several feral kittens, unharmed, shot out of the basket, scattering across the kitchen.

"Mom!" DJ yelled clearly upset with his mother. "Why did you drop them?"

"DJ," Cindy said with an irritated tone, "I didn't know what they were, and you didn't say anything!" Cindy responded.

Immediately she and DJ began dashing around the kitchen, grabbing and searching for loose kittens. DJ explained to Cindy that he had gathered up all the kittens so that they could be given food and care. He was worried about them. DJ begged to keep them all. Dan and Cindy relented, allowing each sibling to keep one.

On another occasion, Cindy was working in the kitchen preparing dinner when she heard DJ yell for her from the back yard. She walked over to the screen door, and there stood her little boy clutching in his hand a spider, "that was the size of his hand." She let out a shriek, immediately ordering DJ to drop the spider.

"Mom," he protested, "I don't want to hurt it."

For Cindy, her son was holding something that potentially could harm him. For DJ, according to his mother, it seemed to be no big deal about the size of the spider. He was far more concerned about no harm coming to the arachnid. After all, it was his duty to protect this small creature. If he didn't do it, who would?

Already detailed in this book are the numerous stories of Danny Dietz the protector. And yet new stories continue to emerge. The stories of adolescent friends being rescued, and a childhood friend who commented, "I always knew he would be there, he would take care of me." Of course there are the stories of Eric and his watchful brother at school and many years later following the car accident. One SEAL teammate wrote that he simply felt better when Danny was around, knowing he would take care of his team.[56] Danny Dietz had a presence, a way about him that put people at ease. They simply knew he was the loyal protector who would take care of what needed to be taken care of. Yet the most compelling story of Danny's loyalty as a protector involves the little girl who he once asked of his mother to "take her back."

Just a few years after the bassinet being pushed over, Danny would demonstrate his loyalty and his protection of Tiffany. Cindy had acquired a part-time job to help with tightening family finances. She had found a daycare, operated by a woman out of her home, to watch the children while she worked. While this new step in life was not her preference, it seemed to be the only step the Dietz family could take.

After dropping the children off for their second day in this new day care, Cindy suddenly had a bad feeling as she drove on to work. She could not explain it, but something just did not feel right about leaving her children. Listening to her gut feeling, she turned her car around and made the trip back to the home-based daycare. Upon arriving, she decided to circle around the house. From the street she could see her two children in the back yard standing in the cold near the back porch door. DJ had wrapped his arms around his little sister, Tiffany. Cindy immediately whipped her car around the corner, pulled into the driveway of the house, and angrily inquired of the lady about the situation. While the lady tried to dismiss the claim, Cindy picked up her children, put them in the car, and quit her part-time job of two days.

Later Danny explained the situation in full: They had wanted some of the cereal the lady was giving to her own grandchild. According to the little boy, the lady refused and put them on the back porch until she had finished feeding the other child. He also shared with his mother that Tiffany had been crying. He had wrapped his arms around her to calm her tears and keep her warm.

Essay Three: A Pledge of Loyalty

In another narrative concerning Danny's sister, often told by Tiffany herself, nine-year-old DJ was riding on the handlebars of his younger sister's bicycle. On this particular afternoon, they found themselves looking down a steep hill. As Tiffany began to ride down the hill, her older brother demanded she not use any brakes. As momentum pulled them down the hill and speed increased, angry and terrified, Tiffany started screaming at the top of her lungs. When they finally came to the bottom of the hill, Tiffany was excited, laughing, and yelling at DJ, "How come you wouldn't let me put the brakes on?"

DJ turned around and looked at her, saying, "Didn't you have fun? Tiff, don't worry, I would never let anything happen to you."

As he sat on the handle bars of that bike, Danny Dietz made a pledge to his sister that he would keep his entire life. The commitment he pledged to her would be lived out a short time later where his loyalty could have potentially brought him great harm.

On a cold Colorado winter morning, DJ and Tiffany were playing in a nearby park. Walking on the outskirts of a frozen river, the two siblings were exploring, when suddenly the frozen ice gave way under Tiffany's feet. Emerged in icy water, Tiffany immediately panicked. Without hesitation, young Danny Dietz threw off his coat and jumped into the river to save his sister. Upon pulling her to safety he wrapped her in his coat to keep her warm.

A pledge fulfilled.

There is a loyalty, a pledge that reaches beyond vow, beyond contract, or allegiance. A loyalty that forfeits self, carries the cross, and willingly makes the ultimate sacrifice for the well-being of another. The stories above do not simply demonstrate a pledge of loyalty. They express a commitment in boyhood that is so great one is willing to give up his own life for another In his song "If I Stand" artist Rich Mullins writes the words, "There's a loyalty that's deeper than mere sentiments." That is the loyalty about which I write. Make no mistake about it. The highest form of such an attachment, for which it is difficult to find words to express, is defined by that Sunday school teacher, in Esssay One of this section, who quoted another who willingly gave His life. It was Jesus Christ who reminded us that, "No greater love hath he, than to lay down his life for his brothers."

I return to the previous story of sitting in Coronado, California, with the unnamed naval captain. As we talked I mentioned that I often use a phrase "You can teach skill, but you cannot train will." I inquired whether he had found that to be true when training Navy SEALs. His answer was short and to the point, "I will take a guy out here that may not run a mile as fast as another, but I know he has the ability to die for his team. I can teach the guy to run faster, I can't teach someone to die for his team." Then he shared a statement about Danny and his fellow teammates on their final mission that to this day when I ponder it, chills my soul. "Make no mistake about it, those men up there, yes, they died serving their country. But in those mountains of Afghanistan, they died for each other as well,"

Pledged to a warrior ethos, devoted to each other, Danny and his Navy SEALs demonstrate to us a "loyalty to Country and Team [that is] beyond reproach."

Essay Four: A Moment's Notice

So there they were, three men traveling across the Nevada desert. Danny Dietz had just completed BUD/S and found himself in a truck with his father, Dan, and life-long friend Howard Weese. Some weeks earlier, Howard had planned to make the journey west and pick up a boat and bring it back to Colorado. Dan Dietz had decided to join Howard on the trip, and together they would bring Danny back for his short break following BUD/S.

As they made the trip, the boat trailer lights continued to give issue, seldom blinking off and on. Eventually, the lights snapped off, leaving the trailer without proper signaling. As they made their way down the highway, local tow truck services searching for work began honking their horns attempting to get the gang of three to pull over. Eventually, one truck driver who continually taunted the trio was successful in getting them to pull the truck and boat to the curb. Weese, driving the vehicle, pulled over not so much because of the honking, but to see if he could get the lights to work. The tow truck had been annoyingly taunting and harassing them for some time.

Without hesitation Danny looked at Howard and honestly asked, "You want me to take care of this?" For Danny it was not a question to flex his muscle or show his strength. Nor was he attempting to be a bully. Danny was simply ready to protect those around him.

Loyalty demands a person, in a moment's notice, to react to a commitment or protection of a person or organization. Back in chapter one I wrote about the story of Danny's threatening kids to never pick on his kid brother again. In a moment's notice, he acted. When the charm bracelet broke and fell down the mountain, as told in chapter three, without thought he bound down the mountain to retrieve it. In a moment's notice, he acted. When the car was sinking in the river and his friends were inside, he jumped into the water with little thought. In a moment's notice, he acted.

Did he have the courage to act? Yes. Dedication to those involved? Absolutely.

In different conversations and in reading different postings about Danny Dietz, the words "quintessential team guy" or "consummate Navy SEAL" are used. Meaning, he lived the ethos; he was loyal and would act in a moment's notice for a fellow Navy SEAL. On one occasion, a Navy SEAL team guy, who never gave his name nor told the story, walked up to Dan Dietz Sr., shook his hand, and simply said, "Your son saved my life." In reading and hearing different accounts of Danny as a Navy SEAL, I am continually taken back to the Old Testament story of Joshua. Like Joshua, like all Navy SEALS, Danny at a moment's notice was ready to lead or be led. Before his progression into the leadership position once held by the now-deceased Moses, Joshua had proven himself as someone who was ready to lead. For nearly four decades, Joshua had observed Moses' leadership in the good times and the bad. He had watched as Moses had moved this great army toward the Promised Land and the challenges he had overcome. Because of his faithful protection of Moses, never once had Joshua openly challenged Moses or attempted to thwart his leadership. Now the torch was being passed to Joshua, and he was ready to lead. In the Old Testament book of Joshua, the God of Israel tells the new leader that now is his moment. Nothing is recorded about Joshua's refusing, fearing, or doubting his step from being led to being the leader. He acted in a moment's notice. Just as before, he remained loyal to his people, his countrymen, and faithful to his God as he accepts this great responsibility.

Stories of Danny's as a Navy SEAL leadership have inspired current Navy SEALs in their career. Many of the same stories have inspired other young men to pursue being the best of the best. Even as this book is being written, a young man who has been inspired by Danny's leadership is stepping into the BUD/S program. However, when Danny became a leader, he always knew what it was to be led. Treating those with or without rank the same, Danny would listen and allow others to lead him. His respect for all people translated into his ability to follow the leadership of others. And this he did, in a moment's notice, with what appears to be little struggle. Even on that fateful day in the Hindu Kush Mountains, Danny was willing to be led. Only the strongest of leaders can be led by others.

In a speech to the Reserve Officers Association, then-President George W. Bush said, "Because of the courage of Petty Officers Axleson and Dietz, their wounded teammate made it out alive."[57] Like Joshua of the Bible, driven by loyalty never once did Danny hesitate in his position, whether he was a follower or a leader.

Medallion Moment

When it comes to loyalty, it is difficult for me not to think of making a pledge. We all make pledges in one form or another. I am pledged to my wife. I sign contracts with organizations, pledging to render public speaking services. I raise my hand over my heart and pledge allegiance to the American flag. With loyalty comes a pledge.

After all, when the SEAL ethos is analyzed, it is a pledge. And to that pledge these great warriors remain loyal. When reading, hearing of, and then writing about the pledged loyalty of Danny Dietz, I could not help but think of another great warrior; he too had a pledge. He too, like Danny, characterized the very spirit of loyalty.

His name was Martin Treptow. A male barber by trade, he volunteered with the Iowa National Guard in 1917. Leaving that hometown barbershop, Martin soon found himself in the 168th Infantry of the 42nd, Rainbow Division. While in Europe fighting the "war to end all wars," World War I, Martin volunteered for his last assignment. A major battle began to draw to a finish, and a request was made for a messenger to carry an extremely important message to another platoon. Without hesitation, driven by his courage and loyalty to his division, Private Martin Treptow snagged the message, placing himself in the heat of heavy fire as he moved toward his destination. As he reached the platoon, Martin was cut down by a hail of enemy fire. The story, however, does not end there.

Later, after search and recovery, when Martin's personal belongings were being collected, they found on his person a blood-stained diary. Upon opening the journal, they discovered an entry, written in Treptow's handwriting. He entitled the writing, "My Pledge." Under that heading he inscribed:

> America shall win the war.
>
> Therefore, I will work. I will save.
>
> I will sacrifice. I will endure.

> I will fight cheerfully and do my utmost, as if
> the whole issue of the struggle depended on me
> alone.[58]

In that writing, Martin Treptow demonstrates the pledge of loyalty to his nation, his team, and his belief in the importance of freedom. I want to take this medallion moment, to write to the cause for which Martin Treptow, Danny Dietz, and so many others have given—freedom. I would almost be remiss in a book honoring a fallen warrior to not mention liberty and a calling to remain loyal to that cause. As previously written, loyalty is a devoted attachment, so let us be attached with great devotion to the cause of freedom and human rights here and around the world. This leads me to a portion of speech delivered by former president Ronald Reagan.

Standing on the northern shore of France, with the wind blowing on that overcast day, President Reagan spoke of freedom brought about by loyalty. As the president later showed signs of tearful sorrow, he declared the following words to commemorate the fortieth anniversary of the Normandy Invasion, where thousands died to end World War II:

> These are the boys of Pointe du Hoc. These are
> the men who took the cliffs. These are the cham-
> pions who helped free a continent. These are the
> heroes who helped end a war.
>
> Gentlemen, I look at you and I think of the
> words of Stephen Spender's poem. You are men
> who in your "lives fought for life...and left the
> vivid air signed with your honor..."

> Forty summers have passed since the battle that you fought here. You were young the day you took these cliffs; some of you were hardly more than boys, with the deepest joys of life before you. Yet you risked everything here. Why? Why did you do it? What impelled you to put aside the instinct for self-preservation and risk your lives to take these cliffs? What inspired all the men of the armies that met here? We look at you, and somehow we know the answer. It was faith, and belief; it was loyalty and love.
>
> The men of Normandy had faith that what they were doing was right, faith that they fought for all humanity, faith that a just God would grant them mercy on this beachhead or on the next. It was the deep knowledge—and pray God we have not lost it—that there is a profound moral difference between the use of force for liberation and the use of force for conquest. You were here to liberate, not to conquer, and so you and those others did not doubt your cause. And you were right not to doubt.[59]

As a nation, as a people, we have always been loyal to the cause of liberty, of freedom, of human rights. Reagan asked and answered the question of why the warrior does what the warrior does—out of loyalty and love for freedom. President John Kennedy, standing in cold air of January 1961, made it clear how America views liberty when he said:

> Let every nation know, whether it wishes us well or ill, that we shall pay any price, bear any burden, meet any hardship, support any friend, oppose any foe to assure the survival and the success of liberty.[60]

And so it is today. Make no mistake, those who have fallen in battle did so out of loyalty to a flag, the belief in the rights of all men, and the love for the life of liberty that we should so cherish. Like Danny Dietz, let us do what we must in a moment's notice to protect this freedom in which we have been trusted.

_____

_____

_____

_____

Section Seven

Nine and Never Out: When All You Have Is All You Have

A coward dies a thousand deaths…a soldier dies but once.

—William Shakespeare

I cannot fathom the emotional torment and even the physical pain of a parent whose military child is missing in action. Nor can I imagine the grief of hearing the news that your military child who was once classified missing in action is now classified killed in action. Therefore, there are no medallion moments in this section of essays. There is very little we can learn from the events you will read. My only hope is that through the essays we can experience just a tiny fraction of what all Gold Star parents' experience. That from this section, every time we see the phrase, "Freedom is not free," we will grasp just how small that statement is in comparison to the reality.

Essay One: The Death of the Typical, the Ordinary, and the Normal

It was a typical day. June 28, 2005 was an ordinary sunny Colorado summer day. Cindy Dietz and her daughter, Tiffany, were running around town checking off a list of normal errands. Driving along in the mild afternoon sun, Cindy received a phone call. There had been an "incident" involving Navy SEALs in a downed helicopter; there was little information, and Danny's direct involvement could not be confirmed. As a Blue Star parent with children actively serving in the military, it is not abnormal to receive such a phone call. Information leaks or news source reports of an unordinary incident involving a certain unit or branch of the military and the dreaded curiosity begins: *Is my loved one involved?* Cindy reassured Tiffany that DJ was probably just fine. There was not enough information to even begin to worry. Nonetheless, Cindy decided to phone Dan with the unconfirmed news.

During a workday, Dan would typically hear from Cindy. Seeing her cell phone number on his caller ID was nothing out of the ordinary. However, as he answered his wife's call, Dan Dietz Sr. had no idea what he was about to hear. As he drove down a street in Littleton, Colorado, Dan listened as Cindy explained the phone call she had received. While a helicopter containing Navy SEALs had gone down in the mountains of Afghanistan, there was no confirmation of Danny's involvement. Dan began peppering her with normal questions, for which she had no answer. What Cindy did know was that if something were wrong with their son, the Navy would come visit them at their home.

To this day, Dan Sr. is unable to describe the sickening feeling that overcame him. An overwhelming sensation of anxiety suddenly ravaged his mind. He thought he could go about his day until there was more information but he was wrong. Consumed by images of his son, Dan u-turned his Power Wagon truck to return to their home. While his hope was to catch some cable news, his fear was that a United States Navy vehicle would be sitting in his driveway. The short drive home on this particular day seemed to exaggerate time as Dan kept mumbling to himself, though unsubstantiated, "This is not good, this is not good." He had a brief moment of reprieve when he rounded his neighborhood street corner to find no vehicles sitting in front of his house.

A few moments later Cindy arrived home, finding Dan on the front porch. He was pacing with nervous-ridden energy, and his face communicated only one message: fear. As she and Tiffany walked up the steps, Cindy and Dan briefly conversed that neither had new information. Cable news was blaring from the front room television announcing that a helicopter caring military personnel had been shot down in the mountains of Afghanistan. Cindy walked on through the front door and began unpacking her shopping bags. Dan remained on the front porch as though on lookout. Praying that he would not see any US Navy personnel pull into his driveway, he instead hoped that Cindy's phone would ring with new information announcing that all was fine with their son.

Quickly, that hope would be crushed.

As Dan Sr. watched from the front porch, a blue jeep clearly marked with a United States Navy decal passed his house. This is the moment that every parent of an active military warrior cannot and does not ever want to fathom. All Dan could think was, *Oh no.* The sickening feeling that hit him earlier in the day following Cindy's call paled in comparison to the empty pit he now felt forming in his stomach. Since they had passed his house, a little glitter of hope remained that maybe it was merely a coincidence. He knew the odds were slim that the navy personnel were not looking for them; however, any hope was better than the sickening feeling in his soul. That last glimmer of hope was quickly extinguished as he watched the jeep turn around in a neighbor's driveway. He knew this sort of visit was not typical, was not ordinary, and clearly was not normal. Knowing what was about to happen, Dan swallowed hard past the lump in his throat. As the Jeep pulled into the driveway, Dan walked off his porch steps to meet the naval officers. All he could think was, *Please God, no.* "Jeremy, my heart sank," Dan shared in a later interview.

Lieutenant Jon Schaffner, First Officer Jay Martinez, and Navy Chaplain Mary Ann Kehoe emerged from the vehicle wearing their service dress blue uniforms. They walked up the driveway and greeted Dan Sr. A few minutes later, Cindy, daughter Tiffany, and youngest son Eric joined Dan in the driveway. Feeling as though she could not breathe, as though a fifty-pound weight had been strapped to her back, Cindy listened as Lieutenant Schaffner explained what the navy did and did not know about the incident now splashed all across the evening news. They knew for sure that a Chinook CH-47 helicopter had been brought down by enemy combatants in the Hindu Kush Mountains of Afghanistan. He further explained that Danny's presence on the helicopter, his whereabouts, and his physical condition could not now be confirmed. In light of this, Danny Dietz was officially labeled missing in action. Other than knowing that Danny was in the region, they had little other information to share. Yet the MIA classification gave Cindy a glimmer of hope. While the typical, ordinary hours of the earlier part of the day of shopping, of normality seemed to fade into a "forever ago," there was optimism that Danny would be just fine.

As Cindy's daughter Tiffany would later share, "It was just like a movie. It happened just like it does in the movies."

Quickly, all their questions and anxieties turned into a flurry of activity and motion. The family needed to relocate closer to the information sources and news. Dan, Cindy, daughter Tiffany, and son Eric began making preparations to leave Colorado for Virginia Beach, where Danny was stationed. There in Danny's home, along with their daughter-in-law, they would receive information at a faster pace. Knowing their desire to relocate temporarily to Virginia Beach, Lieutenant Schaffner began assisting the family in their travel plans. Flight reservations were quickly made to leave Denver, Colorado, for Virginia Beach the following morning.

The early evening seemed to drag into the night. All the family could do was wait and pray—and then wait some more. Dan and Cindy spoke with extended family and with friends. Hoping of gleaning any bit of information that had potentially leaked, they remained vigilant in their viewing of all cable news. While Lieutenant Schaffner and his team worked on behalf of the family to garner any information possible, at times the evening news offered more information than what the United States Navy could give. As news leaked that a Navy SEAL from Littleton was in trouble, local media outlets, neighbors, and friends began to call on the family. Schaffner asked a member of his team to begin fielding all media inquiries, as the phone continued ringing and local television cameras arrived at the front door of the Dietz home.

All the time through the haze of little information and extreme ups and downs of the moments, Cindy maintained a presence of hope. She refused to believe that DJ was gone. Maybe wounded, but not gone, not dead, not her DJ. "I mean, after all," she later recounted, "he was good at being a Navy SEAL." As well, Dan knew that his son had gotten out of some tight spots before. He even recalled in his thoughts the few stories that were permissible for sharing by Danny. And this feeling of optimism was only bolstered more every time Schaffner would answer his cell phone. Maybe that was the call telling them that Danny had been located safe and sound.

Yet that phone call never came. Unless you have lived it, I doubt many can imagine the experience of hearing that your child has been in harms way as a warrior and is now classified mission in action. There are no words to adequately describe the emotional turmoil that borders on torment that a Blue Star parent must feel. The next morning they would board flights bound for Virginia Beach. For the Dietz family, morning could not arrive soon enough.

And soon, for this family, the ideas of typical—what is ordinary and everyday, normal living—would be redefined forever.

Essay Two: When Fireworks Grow Dim

By July third, sitting in Virginia Beach more than a week after they had first received news about their son's missing in action, Cindy and Dan Sr. still knew very little about Danny's condition or whereabouts. Nearly a week since learning of the helicopter downing, the family now knew that Danny had been participating in a classified reconnaissance mission in the Hindu Kush of Afghanistan. He had not been on the CH-47 that was shot down. Instead, Danny and his SEAL team had been compromised. A gun battle ensued, and the helicopter that had been brought down by a rocket-propelled grenade was full of brave Army Night Stalkers and Navy SEALs attempting to assist their brothers-in-arms. Earlier in the week the family had been given some major information: at least one SEAL had survived the attack. The navy had released information that a tracking device, located in the boot of one of the Navy SEALs, was on the move. At the word of this information Dan Sr. began to say over and over to himself, *Run, Danny, run*. All they could do, like the parents of the other missing Navy SEALs, was simply hold out prayers and hope. Yet as every day turned into the next, that hope was fading.

Cindy's original optimism was now being crushed with anxiety over the "hush-hush" lack of information from the US Navy. An hourly battle raged in her heart and soul, moving from a flank of worry to hope and outright anxiety. For a few moments she would find peace. At times she would cry. In her heart of hearts she would not, could not, surrender to the notion that DJ was not coming home. Did she fear the worst at times? Of course; she is a mother. Did she accept the worst at this moment? Of course not; she is a mother.

In the meantime, Dan continually reminded himself of how good Danny was at being a Navy SEAL. Before this current deployment Danny had shared with his father his desire to seek a position in development group more commonly known as Team Six. His plans were to follow through on that next step after this current deployment. Dan recounted that since Danny graduated from his training, he had never again called him his boyhood nickname DJ. He was now Danny. Even on his cell phone, representing the family with news reporters and the media, he referred to his son as Danny. All the while Dan kept uttering to himself, "Run, Danny, run! It just has to be you alive."

Over time, many people visited the Dietz family at Danny's Virginia Beach home. Naval Special Warfare community members stopped by to check on the family. Fellow Navy SEAL team guys would visit. Some stayed for hours with the family, while others were there only a few minutes. Some visitors prayed with the family. Others encouraged them. All would make sure that they had anything and everything they wanted or needed. And while eating seemed like a faraway, distant option of the past, visitors still brought trays and dishes of food.

Now several days into the waiting game, anxiety was turning to frustration. Dan and Cindy had both lost significant weight. Sleep only happened when exhaustion won the battle of fatigue. The navy had asked the family not to watch media reports. With the television off, the family waited to hear about Danny, experiencing a cover of mixed, contradictory, and overwhelming emotions that created a solemn atmosphere. This subdued and somber mood only gave way when Commander Wilson, assigned to provide information to the family, approached the front door offering any news available. In those brief few seconds, hope would abound. Yet in just a few moments, the hope would fade as the only news given was no new news. *Why did they not know more about Danny? Was he alive? Was he hurt? Captured? They still had no information all of these days later!* At times, hope and belief morphed to desperation and tearful prayers.

All of this fear and anxiety did not melt away as the Virginia sun welcomed the July Fourth celebration of Independence Day. The Dietz family had little to celebrate. Their son, on behalf of independence, was missing. Mind you, there was no bitterness. On that national holiday celebrating freedom, there was no bitterness against liberty or angst towards America. Danny was doing exactly that for which he was destined. There was just the longing to know he was alive.

Throughout this particular Independence Day, as in other days, there was a fog of news reports, speculation, and continuous wondering of the lone tracking device running through the mountains of Afghanistan. The US Navy still would not release the name of the SEAL to which that boot belonged. Several more days had passed since the tracking device was located, and for several days the Navy would not comment on it. While the world seemed to stop turning for the Dietz family, outside the walls of their son's Virginia Beach home the Fourth of July celebrations rolled on. The smells of barbeques, hot charcoals, and firework sulfur filled the air with noises of pops, crackles, and bangs, mixed with laughter leading a chorus of celebration. It was all too strange for both Dan and Cindy.

Through that surreal mixture of early evening celebrations, Commander Wilson once again approached the front door. As typical for the family, they all gathered in Danny's living room to await any news. This time as Commander Wilson crossed the home threshold, there was a difference in his demeanor. He looked at the family, dropped his head for a second, and then looked at them and simply said, "I'm sorry. Danny is no longer with us."

At just twenty-five years of age, Danny P. Dietz, United States Navy SEAL was gone.

Time suddenly stood still. For a split second nobody moved. No sounds were made. It was though the room had been frozen, the sound ripped out, and the only noises that were audible were the fireworks, now eerie in their display of freedom. In the next split second, doubt and denial filled the air as heads shook from side to side. This was not how the story was to end! This once little three-year-old boy who yearned for a punching bag and wanted to be a cowboy at age five was not done living. After all, he still had goals to achieve, dreams to reach, and life to live. He was only twenty-five! *No, no, no! Danny, DJ could not be dead! It must be a mistake! He is still alive. He just has to be alive!* As denial succumbed to reality in the next split second, the room became filled with the sounds of ultimate, devastating grief. Overbearing, unimaginable grief soon overtook the sounds of firecrackers and " the rockets red glare."

There was a gasp for air. And the harder Cindy tried to breathe, the more fleeting the oxygen became. The room began to shake and then spin. Her once little boy who became a Navy SEAL was dead. Outside she could hear the blasted fireworks of the national holiday exploding. Her son was gone. *Boom*. Her heart felt as though it were going to implode. *Crack*. The fireworks continued to sound as though tauntingly celebrating the execution of her oldest child. *Fizzle*. He was supposed to be the one alive. *Snap*. He was supposed to walk through that door with that crooked smile acting as if nothing ever happened. *Another boom*.

Why, God why? Overcome by emotion, Cindy began to feel her knees weaken. And in a split second, as another firework displayed its reds and blues through the living room window, Cindy could no longer support her own body weight. Her knees buckled. The room went black. Fainting, she fell to the floor.

With the assistance of a naval doctor who had accompanied Commander Wilson, Dan helped Cindy to a back bedroom bed. He stood there for a few moments, looking down at her, feeling nothing but numbness. As the doctor finished an examination, Dan Sr., with a face drawn from sorrow and eyes bloodshot with grief, walked onto Danny's back porch. There he found his youngest son Eric, a stunning resemblance to Danny, looking down at the ground. As Dan walked through the sliding door, Eric looked up at his father. And Eric's face, a forever remembrance of Danny, communicated one word—anger; his eyes were full of rage.

Dan stood there looking at the evening sky, still filled with sounds of bottle rockets and sparklers.

Dan felt the anger too. "We can't let this anger, this rage destroy us, Eric. We have to channel this rage, this feeling into something good, something positive. That's what Danny would have wanted."

Eric did not respond. He was in no mood to talk, to have a discussion about anger. Dan looked back up at the evening sky, seeing the nighttime stars poke through the drifting smoke of spent fireworks. Even though he had spoken to Eric what he knew to be true, his soul ached, his mind furiously wondered, *What happened in Afghanistan? How was my son killed, murdered?* Then, before any other questions could dance in his mind, his thoughts drifted back to the naval officer's announcement, "Danny is no longer with us." At that moment he had felt as though he had been punched in the chest, as though all the sound, all the noise had been sucked out of the room and all that he could hear was a far-off ringing sensation in his ears. He remembered trying to speak, trying to move, but all he could muster was to stare back at the naval officer, frozen by shock. Now he stood silent on the day America celebrates the birth of a nation, feeling as though his life had ended.

After Cindy had been revived, those around, including the naval doctor, decided she needed to be examined by a local emergency room physician. The diagnosis was pronounced: exhaustion and malnutrition as the result of losing nearly fifteen pounds in a week. She now only weighed a hundred pounds. Yet the diagnosis had failed to mention a major contributing factor in Cindy's fainting—sorrow. It only takes a split second to become a Gold Star mother. And in that split second moving from a Blue Star mother, having a child actively serving in the armed forces, to a Gold Star mother, having a child who died in active military service, life changes forever.

Cindy lay in the emergency room bed, looking up at the ceiling. While she was not thinking about the split-second journey that had just been forced upon her, she lay there thinking about DJ and his journey. One moment she remembered the little boy who would protect a kitten. The next moment she thought of his smile, his laugh. There were moments of terror, wondering what his final minutes in Afghanistan brought. She tearfully hoped, sobbing that he had not suffered pain. She reminisced about the last time she saw him alive during the previous Christmas Holiday. She hugged him before he left to return to Virginia Beach. How she wished, how she longed to reach up on her tiptoes one more time, wrap her arms around his neck, and squeeze. She closed her eyes and wept.

Essay Three: When the Flag Returned from Half Mast

Following the joint memorial service in Virginia Beach and subsequent funeral conducted in Danny's final resting place, Colorado, life for Dan and Cindy Dietz shattered. When the media cameras left and friends and family had paid their final respects, they were simply left with each other. Cindy entered a period, common for Gold Star mothers, of dark depression. She had little energy for anything in life. Down the hall from her bedroom was a closet full of memories. His clothes, his old Tae Kwon Do trophies, his numerous art pads full of drawings were waiting to remind her of his twenty-five years on this earth. All she wanted to do, daily, was sift through Danny's belongings, clinging to them in quiet sorrow. She would look at the different memories in her hands and sob.

Dan Sr. dealt with the grief in his own way—a search for truth to what happened on June 28, 2005. He had questions, indignant and justified questions, to which there were no answers. He sought, he pushed, and even at times demanded: *What happened on that day? What happened to my son?* He could not focus on work, and with any other employer he would have probably lost his job. Yet the owners of Brown Brothers Asphalt and Concrete, his place of work, grieved with him, offering encouragement, assistance, and time away. (Later on, company owners Dennis and Ami Brown would receive a letter from the secretary of the navy commending them for their support of the fallen warrior's father.) Dan prayed for the soul of peace that continually evaded him, yet he sought the truth about Operation Red Wings and what had happened in those mountains.

Dan and Cindy grieved separately. They grieved in their own way—apart from each other. The summer of 2005 turned to autumn. The leaves turned colors and fell to the ground. Yet the leaves went without being raked at the Dietz home, falling to grass that badly needed mowed. A few minor projects on the house went undone or unfinished as Dan slipped into the "darkest period of [his] life."

Even one night late, after returning to his job, he sat in his work truck and experienced something to this day he cannot explain. As he sat there, not driving, the complete life of his son flashed before his eyes. He saw images from Danny's birth to the last time he was home in Colorado. Dan broke down, sobbing, weeping with tears that he had never imagined possible.

In the two years that followed Danny's death, the couple was enamored by media requests, attending events, and heavily involved in projects honoring their son. The marriage—shredded by grief, swept up in the business of memorializing, with two people grieving separately and in their own ways, compounded by the neglect that often comes from focusing all energies on raising children—came unraveled. Two years after their son's death, Cindy and Dan separated. Several months later, the divorce was final.

In an interview about those devastating times, both Dan and Cindy openly shared what took place. And, quite frankly, what took place with them is not uncommon among Gold Star families.

"We never thought [through the years of marriage] about working on 'us,'" Cindy shared. "I came to a point where I just wanted to run. I wanted to run away from the memories, I wanted to run away from Dan, from Tiffany and Eric, and I wanted to run away from it all. I just could not deal with it all anymore. It took me a year to realize how badly I needed my children. I also realized I needed Dan, not as my husband, but as a friend. He and I simply no longer knew each other. We were grieving so differently."

Sitting in the same interview, Dan Dietz shook his head in agreement. "Jeremy, Cindy and I put all of our effort, our energy in raising kids. I mean we scrimped and saved and sacrificed everything for our three kids. In doing that, we didn't build 'us' as a couple. Cindy gave up a potential career in insurance. I gave up my dream of working in medicine. And when the kids began moving out, we had an empty nest, our job was done, and it was only compounded more by Danny's death. We hadn't given anything to ourselves, and we didn't know how to grieve together."

Since the time of Danny's passing, Cindy and Dan have experienced a roller coaster of emotions ranging from anger to obvious sorrow to sometimes outright guilt. All of that normal. All of that difficult. Yet today, Dan and Cindy have found some peace.

"We have a purpose," Dan shared. "We have a purpose of sharing Danny, his character, his courage, his bravery with other family and other kids. There are kids out there right now who are headed down the same path Danny was, who need to hear his amazing story of turning his life around and becoming a Navy SEAL."

"My purpose," Cindy interposed, "is that as well, but my larger purpose is being a mother to Tiffany and Eric, a grandmother to my grandchildren, a wife to Don [Cindy recently remarried] and a friend to Dan. I cannot put 100 percent of my energy into DJ's memory, though at times I feel as though I do. But I can't, cause I have learned if I do, it will drive me right back into depression. I have had to learn to live life without DJ."

As with all fallen warriors, the American flag is lowered to half-mast in honor of their sacrifice. Eventually, that flag returns to the top of the pole. America moves on. People continue their lives. Yet for a Gold Star family, life is never the same. While life has continued, it has and never will completely move on, not without Danny. Together, Dan and Cindy appear at events bearing the name of their Navy SEAL son, other events for the families of fallen warriors, and other numerous honorable functions. Occasionally they entertain a speaking engagement talking about Danny, his virtue, and his life. They answer the phone when local media outlets call requesting a comment after any incident involving anything Navy SEAL. And every time they embark on these works or see Old Glory at the top of her mast billowing in the Colorado sun, the peace they have found is strengthened. They know he is gone. But his spirit of freedom that gave all it had on behalf of freedom continues.

Essay Four: Mr. President

A lot has been written and said about President George W. Bush. Even as this is being penned, through a very moving ceremony, the former chief executive completed the dedication of his presidential center and library. We will leave history to judge the policies and ideals of the Bush administration. Yet, whatever history may or may not record about President George W. Bush, it will have to accurately account, without fault or error, that as president he dearly loved the American soldier and their families. Previously untold stories continue to emerge about George W. Bush, about his countless visits with wounded soldiers, his prayers with them, and unchecked time spent with their families. This dedication cannot be understated and quite frankly is to be admired. The Dietz family has their own story concerning President Bush. For in a period of real darkness, for just a few hours, he provided light and hope.

In the fall of 2006 the White House contacted the family. President George W. Bush wanted to meet with them privately. The family would not make the trip to Washington, he, the commander-in-chief, was coming to them. In writing about this story I did a quick Google search about President Bush's meeting with the Dietz family. I found a small clipping from the local Denver news. As well, I found a brief press statement, following the meeting, from then Press Secretary Tony Snow aboard Air Force One in route to Texas:

> Mr. Snow: Let me begin just with a couple of details; we will get you the readout on the President's meeting with the family of a fallen sailor in a minute.

From here, Mr. Snow yields to questions concerning the headlines of the day. The brief press conference ended with the following statement:

> Mr. Snow: Okay. Just a read out on the family of the fallen soldier. The President met with the family of Petty Officer 2nd Class, Navy SEAL Danny Dietz, of Littleton, Colorado. He was killed on June 28, 2005, while conducting counter-terrorism operations in Kunar province, Afghanistan. The President went in with members of the Dietz family—the father, Danny

Dietz, Sr., Cindy Dietz, Tiffany Bitz, the sister, and Eric Dietz, the 20-year-old brother. Eric ran the Marine Corps Marathon on October 29th in honor of his brother, Danny. *They went into a room together and it was a completely private moment, no staff present.* Anything else we need here? (emphasis added)[61]

And that was all that was said by the White House. Why does this bear mentioning? There is no historical recording of the meeting, outside of a local news story, the above statement, and the photos taken by the Dietz family on their personal cameras. No media. No White House staff. A White House photographer did not enter the room until summoned by the president so that pictures could be taken for the family. It was just the president, the Dietz family, and Lieutenant Schaffner.

George W. Bush wanted it that way.

Dressed in an open color shirt and sport coat, he spent a significant amount of time with the family. He hugged them, cried with them, posed for pictures, asked how they were doing, and then asked what he could do to help or serve them. They responded with a minor request. He promised to deliver on his word. And in fact, later he kept his word. He gave them a direct line to reach him, if there was ever anything he could do for them. Cindy would use that phone number only once. And the direct line was exactly that, a direct line past all typical White House operator protocol.

He presented the family with a coin bearing the seal of the American presidency. In turn, Dan and Cindy Dietz presented him with the Danny Dietz challenge coin. He said that one day that coin would maintain a presence in his presidential library. And knowing the president, it someday will. The Dietz family supported this president and, even with the loss of their son, supported and believed in America's efforts in the War on Terror. After all, Danny was in Florida undergoing training for his SEAL career during the attacks of September 11, 2001.

Sometime later, Cindy would meet with President Bush again—this time with a group of Gold Star mothers in the Oval Office at the White House. The president hugged her, asking about her other two children by name, recalling facts and conversation pieces from their original meeting. President Bush has been a light of hope for this family. His genuine compassion and sincere care spoke into the hearts of Dan Sr. and Cindy. This section of essays, this book would not be complete without mentioning it.

George W. Bush has a profound respect for our military, the fallen soldier, and he simply loves the Gold Star families. In sharing about the encounter with President Bush, Dan Dietz spoke frankly, "He's a good man. He spent a lot of time with us. There is no doubt that he genuinely cared and still does to this day."

Essay Five: Nine and Never Out of the Fight

Nine. That is the number of bullets, the number of wounds, which Danny P. Dietz took in the line of battle. None of the nine wounds were given at close range. Reports state that he took up to five bullets and continued to defend his fellow SEAL teammates, providing cover fire for escape, and he continually stayed behind. Recently there have been different views, opinions, and research done that offer potentially different and sometimes conflicting accounts of what happened on June 28, 2005. Here is what we know and the Dietz family maintains:

Gunner's Mate 2nd Class (SEAL) Danny P. Dietz is an American hero who valiantly fought and gave his life for his fellow SEAL teammates and for the cause of freedom. The actions demonstrated by Sonar Technician 2nd Class (SEAL) Matthew Gene Axelson, Lieutenant Michael P. Murphy (SEAL), Petty Officer 1st Class (SEAL) Marcus Luttrell during Operation Red Wings were heroic.

The four-man team that was in the mountains of Afghanistan on June 27 to 28 of 2005 was outnumbered with a positional disadvantage. During the fierce gun battle that ensued, Danny stayed behind more than once to provide cover fire for his fellow teammates. Excerpts of Danny's citation for Navy Cross state that:

> Petty Officer Dietz demonstrated *extraordinary heroism* in the face of grave danger...
>
> Demonstrating *exceptional resolve* and fully understanding the gravity of the situation and his responsibility to his teammates, Petty Officer Dietz *fought valiantly* against the numerically superior and positionally advantaged enemy force. *Remaining behind in a hailstorm of enemy fire*, Petty Officer Dietz was wounded by enemy fire. Despite his injuries, he bravely fought on, valiantly defending his teammates and himself in a harrowing gunfight, until he was mortally wounded.

By his undaunted courage in the face of heavy enemy fire, and absolute devotion to his teammates, Petty Officer Dietz will long be remembered for the role he played in the Global War on Terrorism.

Petty Officer Dietz's courageous and selfless heroism, exceptional professional skill, and utmost devotion to duty reflected great credit upon him and were in keeping with the highest traditions of the United States Naval Service. He gallantly gave his life for the cause of freedom.

In addition to losing Danny and two other members of the SEAL team assisting with Operation Red Wings, America lost eight additional SEAL team members and eight Army Night Stalkers in their brave attempt to assist their fellow brothers:

FCC (SEAL/SW) Jacques J. Fontan
ITCS (SEAL) Daniel R. Healy
LCDR Erik S. Kristensen (SEAL)
ET1 (SEAL) Jeffery A. Lucas
LT Michael M. McGreevy, Jr. (SEAL)
QM2 (SEAL) James E. Suh
HM1 (SEAL) Jeffrey S. Taylor
MM2 (SEAL) Shane E. Patton
SSG Shamus O. Goare
CWO3 Corey J.
SGT Kip A. Jacoby
SFC Marcus V. Muralles
MSG James W. Ponder III
MAJ Stephen C. Reich

SFC Michael L. Russell
CWO4 Chris J. Scherkenbach

June 28, 2005 also demonstrated the darkness of the enemy Danny faced. As evil attempted to reign down, Danny Dietz valiantly and without hesitation waded into its very depths. And with those virtues intact that he had learned as a boy, he gave his life's last breath for his team, for his country. Like so many other warriors during the War on Terror, Danny stood as one good man who would not allow such evil to prevail. Danny Dietz was the very essence of a Navy SEAL, proclaiming to the darkness of wrong, "Not on my watch." In the final moments of Danny's life, he demonstrated virtue that had taken a lifetime to mold.

After the gun battle, a rumor that cannot be proven or denied emerged and made its way to Dan Dietz Sr. The rumor states that once Danny P. Dietz was finally killed, after many wounds, the enemy celebrated. They believed, according to this unproven rumor, they had killed a great warrior. Indeed, they barely had.

As was the case for his entire life, Danny Dietz did not run from this final fight. Those who knew him best are not surprised. His life had led every step of the way to those very final moments in the mountains of Afghanistan. In the opinion of this author, as Danny continually pulled the trigger of his M4, I believe he understood the severity of the situation. With that stare, that calm and collect manner, Danny gave all that he had and then gave a little more.

He was indeed the ultimate warrior.

He was a Navy SEAL.

I heard a voice of the Lord saying, "Whom shall I send, and whom will go for us?" Then said I, "Here I am; send me."

Isaiah 6:8

Section Eight

When Eagles Soar

When he shall die, cut him into little stars,
and he shall make the face of heaven so fond,
that all the word will fall in love with night
and pay no worship to the garish sun.

—William Shakespeare
Romeo and Juliet

The final resting place of Danny Dietz, Fort Logan National Cemetery, Denver, Colorado, is lined with her white stone markers, somberly illustrating just how many fallen warriors this book potentially represents. This place, along with numerous other national cemeteries, is the place of sacred ground. For within her depths lie those represented by the red stripes found on the American flag. And as Lincoln so keenly reminded the people of his day, today we too must remember the "unfinished work" of freedom for "which they who fought…so nobly advanced." In these places marking the cost of freedom, we mourn those we have lost, are reminded of the very high price of war, and must pledge ourselves to continue the mission for which they who lay there so bravely fought.

Each and every funeral of a fallen soldier is solemn and mournful in its own unique way. For Danny the memorial was kept smaller in size by request of the family. Thousands would have attended, had they been allowed. Yet for the family, for family friends, it was their moment to say good-bye to *their* hero. At graveside, there were presentation of flags, a twenty-one-gun salute, and the bugling of taps. Joey Bunch, a Denver Post Staff Writer, recorded that:

> Navy SEAL Danny Dietz returned home Thursday, laid to rest at Fort Logan National Cemetery near his boyhood home in Littleton.
>
> A black carriage drawn by a white horse delivered his flag-draped casket to a memorial worthy of a hero—the release of doves, military men moved to tears, taps moaning from a trumpet as the scent of burned powder from a 21-gun salute wafted in the faint breeze.[62]

And while this place of mourning may very well be the "final resting place" for the fallen SEAL, Danny's story does not end at that grave. At the funeral of this special warrior, something peculiar, miraculous, beyond unique, and jaw dropping took place. There was a special visitor. And in fact, this would not be the only time such an honored visitor would appear.

During the service held at the national cemetery, family members noticed a small shadow from the sun swooping along the ground in various circular patterns. They looked up and to their astonishment found an American Bald Eagle circling. The breathtaking image of the circling eagle seemingly communicated, on behalf of Danny Dietz to his family and friends, the words of John Gillespie Magee's poem:

> Oh, I have slipped the surly bonds of Earth—Put out my hand and touched the face of God.[63]

Two years later, on July Fourth, a memorial sculpture honoring Danny was dedicated in Littleton, Colorado. With over three thousand people in attendance, the statue dedication witnessed uninvited VIP guests—two Bald Eagles circling against the clear blue sky. Two years later, almost to the day, a ten-mile stretch of highway was dedicated honoring this Colorado warrior. As the Dietz family stood there for the unveiling of the sign marking the highway, someone looked up, pointing to the hazy glare of the August sky. There they were, as if on guard duty, eagles circling the ceremonious event.

And all three times that those eagles soared, one cannot help but recall the Old Testament passage as Hosea proclaims:

> I will deliver this people from the power of the grave;
>
> I will redeem them from death.
>
> Where, O death, are your plagues?
>
> Where, O grave, is your destruction?[64]

It was as though God Himself sent the eagles to say, "You can mourn Danny's loss. But your loss is heaven's gain." That while Danny may have grown tired and weary in battle, even stumbling and falling at times, he was now "soaring on wings like an eagle; running and not growing weary; walking and not becoming faint."[65] While other religious systems have proclaimed that soaring eagles touch the face of God, the Old Testament Scriptures proclaim men being "swift as eagles," God bringing His people to Him "on eagles' wings," and of course the Isaiah 40 passage:

Do you not know? Have you not heard?

The Lord is the everlasting God, the Creator of the ends of the earth.

He will not grow tired or weary, and his understanding no one can fathom.

He gives strength to the weary and increases the power of the weak.

Even youths grow tired and weary, and young men stumble and fall; but those who hope in the Lord will renew their strength.

They will soar on wings like eagles; they will run and not grow weary, they will walk and not be faint.[66]

For many centuries eagles have represented the image of strength, majesty, courage, and power. In the case of Danny, the eagles soaring represent that and much more: a work not complete, a virtue that continues on. Fort Logan National Cemetery may be the final resting place of Navy SEAL Danny Dietz, but that grave has not and cannot contain the virtue that was within.

It is the virtue of Danny Dietz, the virtue of all the lost heroes of Operation Red Wings, that continues to inspire millions. Their lives, not deaths, extend to us a different view of living life. We find ourselves challenging our own sense of courage, of integrity, and so forth. For us, how they chose to live in many ways represents the uprightness we want to demonstrate. In short, we look at our dispositions, hoping that we too would make the right call at the right moment, whatever the personal cost.

While many may be inspired, others seemingly inherit the virtue of the warrior who went before them. Most who hear the stories of Danny, or any courageous soldier, are moved emotionally. Yet others give the impression as if they have received a gift, as if somehow a miracle took place and pieces of virtue were left to them by those who have gone before. After all, it is one thing to live in the memory of someone who has passed. It is a different thing altogether to live out their virtue.

Essay Two: Danny from the Desert

She was three years old. And at this ripe age, toddler Avery Heinz was known for her chattiness, especially with her younger brother, Logan, in the back seat of the family car. Those of us who are parents know the familiar sounds of a toddler chatting to themselves or siblings in the back seat. Typically as parents we drive along, smiling with amusement as they describe their latest adventure, interaction with a friend, or numerous facets of wisdom from the mouths of babes. Sometimes we even turn down the car stereo volume just so we can eavesdrop with a smile or soak up the moment of what someday will all too soon be gone. This would never be truer for Dee Heinz as it was on one particular morning.

Driving along Whitney Island, this wife of a navy sailor overheard her daughter telling a story to her younger brother and older sister. A name in the short narrative grabbed her attention, and she immediately turned the volume on the radio down, looking into the rearview mirror. Dee asked Avery what story she was offering on this particular day.

Avery responded, "I am telling Logan and Lauren about Danny from the desert."

Passing along the streets of this military town, three-year-old Avery began telling her mother that while she was in heaven, "before being born," she met Danny from the desert. Dee was shocked. According to Avery, Danny from the desert was a brave man. And this brave man, along with three friends, had been fighting "bad men" in the desert. They fought very hard, little Avery shared, but there were "too many bad men," and eventually Danny from the desert "had to go night-night."

Stunned was the only word to describe this mother of three. Never before had she or her husband mentioned Danny Dietz, Operation Red Wings, or even Navy SEAL to their three-year-old. Why would they?

Avery continued sharing that "eagles came and took Danny to heaven. Jesus met him there and gave him a band-aid for his boo boo, and it won't hurt anymore." Avery added that Danny from the desert had an "ouchie" on his thumb. (One of the numerous wounds Danny sustained in the harrowing gun battle was a thumb injury.) The toddler ended her story on that particular day telling her mother that, "Danny is happy in heaven, but he misses his family."

Dee began to ask additional questions, but Avery stopped talking, stopped sharing information. And this would become a pattern. Avery would begin telling another story about Danny from the desert. She would give specific details, of which she had no prior knowledge. When her mother would begin asking questions, she would simply stop talking. Dee and her husband labeled it the "Danny from the desert zone."

Sometime later, Avery had another "Danny from the desert zone" moment. The little girl began sharing that Danny from the desert had been her big brother in heaven, and they had "played together." Dee began to ask questions, and again Avery stopped talking. Quickly she learned to stop asking questions and wait for Avery to share. On one other occasion Avery detailed a story of Danny from the desert bringing her flowers, a drink, and a card. She explained that the card was for his mother. Avery couldn't recall what the card read, but said if she ever met the mother of Danny from the desert, she might remember.

When Avery was shown a picture of Danny Dietz, without prompting, she recognized him, stating that he indeed was Danny from the desert. She then asked if it could be hung above her bed in her bedroom. "That way he can protect me at night."

In the middle of these different stories, Dee Heinz began to wrangle with the decision of potentially contacting Cindy Dietz-Marsh. Avery wanted to meet the mother of Danny from the desert. And while she was urged by a friend to contact the Gold Star mother, Dee felt strongly about the prospect of bringing any more pain to a family who had lost a son to war. Finally, a group of ladies from Dee's weekly prayer group convinced her, through a mutual contact, to reach out to Cindy Dietz-Marsh about Avery and her relationship with Danny from the desert. Soon after, Dee made the first initial contact to Cindy by e-mail, and regular correspondence began. While Cindy appreci-ated Dee's concerns about not causing her and her fam-ily any more pain, the Gold Star mother was more than excited to meet the special little girl.

Yet before a meeting could be scheduled or Avery even knew the name of Danny from the desert's mom, another story emerged. On one particular evening, Avery had been hard at work on a picture she was drawing. Dee walked over and began inquiring about the crayon-drawn masterpiece. The little girl shared that it was a picture of Danny from the desert. Noticing a female standing next to Danny from the desert in the picture, Avery's mom assumed that Avery had drawn herself. She was informed by her toddler that the picture was of Danny and Cindy.

When I spoke with Dee Heinz and she detailed the different stories printed, I did some double-checking with her. In fact, my exact words to this navy wife were, "Dee, I believe your story, but for a moment I am going to ask some direct, to-the-point, hard questions." I asked if there were ever a time that she and her husband had spoken of Operation Red Wings in front of Avery. Her direct response was that due to the violent content of the story, they would have never spoken of Operation Red Wings. As a parent, I appreciated that answer. I then asked Avery's mother if she and her husband had ever spoken of Danny Dietz in front of Avery. Dee shared that she and her husband had searched through their minds, trying to think of any time they would have mentioned Danny's name. And while they were pretty sure they never had, they were a hundred percent sure they had never spoken about Operation Red Wings or the *Lone Survivor* book by Marcus Luttrell.

Finally the day arrived when little Avery would meet Danny from the desert's mom. Upon the first greeting between Cindy and the toddler, Avery pointed to the Navy SEAL trident necklace that Cindy Dietz-Marsh always wears, saying, "Those were the eagles that carried him to heaven." Avery stood there for a moment, looked back up at Cindy, and simply said, "I miss him."

As tears rolled down her cheeks, Cindy responded, "I miss him too."

Essay Three: Danny and Red Wing Warriors in Pineville

The final battle of Danny Dietz and his teammates and their courage has continually inspired millions. Yet for some, the story pulled them through life-and-death circumstances. In Pineville, North Carolina, we find one such story. Here is the e-mail detailing the events:

> I recently taught a class on preparing for and surviving lethal encounters to a group of law enforcement professionals here in North Carolina. I had asked you in the past for permission to show Danny and his teammates on my computer so everyone here could understand their story. You were so kind to allow me to do that so I incorporated the events of Danny's military service to demonstrate that professionalism and dedication can accomplish great things. Never did I dream that the *Lone Survivor* book would play such an important part not only in the lives of my men

and women but in the life of our own Sergeant Dan Martin.

To make a long story short, Dan and I were reading the book. We both love our country and the men and women who serve it. My family has a military background and I came to law enforcement after serving in the United States Army. In short, we loved the book and it greatly inspired us.

Sergeant Dan Martin is physically fit, meaning he worked out, ate right, the whole nine yards necessary to remain physically healthy and capable. However, one day while in training Sergeant Martin suffered a "widow maker" heart attack. He had an AED [automated external defibrillator] deployed on him nine times but was clinically dead for nearly an hour. Finally, they located only a faint pulse.

The doctors were honest with us and said there was no chance of him making it through this. We were allowed to gather around his bed and talk to him. The heart attack was so severe that his veins had collapsed and his organs had stopped working. For the rest of that day and through most of the night I told him he was on "Murphy's Ridge" and he had to fight, and I meant mad-dog-mean fight. We put a poster on his wall of "Murphy's Ridge" so he could see it.

Well, one hour turned to two hours, which then turned to three hours and so on. For numerous days after that first night we sat with his wife around the clock and finally one day Dan woke up. Sergeant Martin suffered no brain damage or lasting trauma from the heart attack and has since returned to duty. Later Dan said he faintly recalled being given last rights. And he said every time he would hear the harp music he would dig in and fight harder and when the music stopped he would rest until he heard it again. When it was all said and done it wasn't harp music he was hearing but the medical instruments sounding when he would begin to slip away. I give God the credit for his life being spared but he used something we all could understand to do it. With that said, I wanted to share with you what four young brave American warriors did for our Sergeant Dan Martin on 28 June 2005. Their tenacity and courage are still saving lives today.

Dan and I have had many conversations about that book before his heart attack. He warned me that when I got to the end to read it alone and have plenty of tissues handy. He was exactly right and I never knew what your son and his teammates did that day would have such a profound impact on the lives of me and so many others. I pray this helps with your loss and I hope you will always know Danny is a part of this law enforcement organization and the way we train our people.

It is my prayer that this e-mail finds you and your loved ones well. God bless.

William E. Connell Assistant Chief of Police
Pineville Police Department
Pineville, North Carolina

Essay Four: A Marathon

For many of us there was something deep within us that felt seemingly vulnerable, almost shocked, upon hearing the news of actor Christopher Reeve. Superman was hurt, seriously hurt, and for many in 1995 we could not separate the actor from the character. As the story of a horse riding accident unfolded, we began to realize that a man who once seemed unstoppable would be confined to a wheelchair for the rest of his life. Through those events, we became more educated, more knowledgeable about spinal cord injuries. And for the Dietz family, that education would someday be too close to home.

Ten years later, Dan and Cindy Dietz would re-experience this vulnerability, this shock, but this time in their own lives. The previously mentioned car accident involving Eric, their youngest son, which brought Danny home from deployment, still leaves doctors confounded. Several doctors examined the scans taken, only to be speechless. The scans revealed that Eric Dietz had a spinal injury similar to that of Christopher Reeve. According to the experts, Eric Dietz should not be walking and should be confined to a wheelchair. Yet from the story in an earlier essay, one week after Danny Dietz returned to his post, Eric left the hospital. One week after Danny had sat at Eric's bedside whispering in his ear, on his own account and strength Eric walked out of the hospital.

I have only spoken with Eric Dietz a few times. Yet in that brief experience he is without doubt one of the most kind, authentic, gracious, and down-to-earth individuals one can meet. A chef by profession, Eric is extremely analytical and well thought. He carries himself with poise and purpose. When I first met him, I was taken back by the identical resemblance he bears to his brother Danny. Though I never met Danny Dietz, I could not help but think, *Is this what it would have been like to speak with Danny?*

It would only be later that I would hear from Dan Sr. and Cindy about the car accident and Danny's visit to the hospital, Eric's spinal injury, and then the marathon. A marathon. And as the parents detailed the story of the marathon, my mind rushed back to speaking with Eric Dietz. Seemingly, the virtue that Danny held had been passed to his brother.

Not one to brag or have a need for attention, Eric Dietz, one year after being told he may never walk again, ran the annual Marine Corp Marathon. Not only did he run it, he ran it in honor of his Navy SEAL brother. Not only did he run it that day for his brother, his time beat two of Danny's Navy SEAL teammates running the same event. He ran this marathon, all at the same time aspiring to follow in Danny's steps, wear the trident, and become a Navy SEAL. He too longed to live the ethos to which his brother clung. And he might have made the SEAL teams, had it not been for the metal and pins in his neck from the car accident.

We will never know what Danny kept whispering in Eric's ear in the hospital room. And without becoming too sensational, one year later, as if eagles were soaring again, Danny seemed to whisper in his brother's ear one more time. Eric's triumph is Eric's triumph. Make no mistake about that. And the Dietz family credits God with his miraculous medical comeback. (To this day, doctors are still without answer.) Yet they cannot help but ponder what part Danny played in the process as he whispered in his brother's ear. And while Eric is his own person, his battle back from his hospital bed to running that marathon became a living picture of the grit, tenacity, and virtue of his older brother.

A Final Medallion Moment

The most sobering thought as a parent, as a man, is that how I live my life may very well set a pattern for my children, and even my children's children. And yet does not virtue, the way of living, become something passed from family member to family member, generation to generation? Does not how we live our lives become a predictor, a pattern for how those who come behind us shall conduct their own days? Are we not able to break the chains of that which snare us only to live out a better virtue, thereby giving the younger something in which to follow?

We began this book with the premise that the best way to honor the sacrifice of the fallen warrior is to live a life of virtue worthy of his or her sacrifice. We close with that same thought. Knowing that the stories of Danny Dietz, of many other warriors, and the virtues they displayed teach us one thing: the way we live out our lives will impact nameless generations to come. And such an impact, as it was with Navy SEAL Danny Dietz, will only come from one guiding compass—our virtue within.

Author Afterword

Four Principles to Consider

There are two educations. One should teach us how to make a living and the other how to live.

—John Adams

In working with Dan and Cindy, we wanted to not only create a book that preserved the stories of their son's youth, but also offered inspiration from which Americans could draw. I wanted the reader to re-visit some of the very virtues that have made this nation exceptional. In addition, we wanted to help others learn from Danny's life lessons and understand the potential of making life-changing decisions.

As we began the journey to focus on Danny's growing-up years, I quickly realized just how much he, and all special operators, teach us about living. At times, my heart was so deeply touched by the stories of this warrior, and the lives of all special operators, that I knew we had to draw more from those narratives than just memories. It was not my intent to create a self-help book from the life of a fallen warrior. Nor did I simply want to fill time and space with stories, albeit great stories of a great warrior. In essence, I wanted people to see the power of virtue, of decisions, and of living life well. In turn, maybe readers would also create an ethos by which to live.

Early in my writing I embarked upon the journey of helping the reader of this book create their own ethos statement. It simply did not work. The writing felt forced, phony, and ineffective. However, quite by accident, the process of creating an ethos took on new meaning.

Separate from this book, my wife and I, the parents of two little girls, began discussing the idea of creating and drawing up a values list by which our family would live and operate. The goal was to help shape and mold our two daughters based upon that which we believe. We wanted to begin helping them learn the process of making good decisions. Through the process, our hope was that they would grasp the wisdom that all decisions have consequences.

I sat down at my computer and went to work. I began to articulate the values we as parents hold dear. No system. No method. So I thought.

After I finished my work, I shared them with my wife, Christina. From there, with a few additions, the list seemed complete. A few weeks would pass, and she and I would develop three simple overarching rules for our daughters, based from the seven values listed. I developed a graphic, illustrating that sometimes the road less traveled is the road one should take. Once again, all of this was done with no system, no method, so I thought.

I thought wrong.

When we think about it, most of us have a value system by which we choose to live. It may not be that which we want to admit or even a value system we want, but we have one. All we did was begin to put down on paper those values by which we wanted to live or had already been living. Yet putting a group of ideals or values on a paper does not make it an ethos. Year after year, organizations, churches, and individuals create value statements. They will invest time and resources to list values. After they have been placed on a blog, a website, or the refrigerator at home, they are often forgotten—never to be viewed again.

That is not an ethos. That is a waste of time. Ethos, a Greek word, actually means "character, a custom or habit."[67] An ethos is that which gives guidance to a person, an organization, or even a country through beliefs and ideals that directly impact decisions and actions. One must often return to that ethos. We have to review it, teach it, make benchmarks, and slowly it becomes part of who we are.

For our family, our values go far beyond character. Posted in our kitchen on a huge poster, the statements clearly define who we are. They are not statements of hope; they are statements of reality. When people walk through our door, we are telling them this is how we do life in our home. For that matter, every time we see the seven phrases, have a dinner conversation about one, or a moment of discipline with our children, we are once again reminded of what molds us, shapes us, and drives how we live life.

For us, this came as a necessity. For us, it came by accident. When I look back, two different items drove the process for us. The first was our abiding faith in Jesus Christ, plain and simple. The second was the process of this book, writing Danny's stories and continually seeing the ideals that drove him. I wanted that for me. I wanted that for my family.

So I sat down at my computer to begin our process with no system or no method. So I thought. When I look back, I can now see a few principles that guided the way in creating our seven statement family ethos. And when I think of Danny, these four principles come to life:

1. An ethos is often a compilation of ideals/values already being lived.
2. An ethos is something that drives and foundations a person.
3. An ethos calls us to a larger life.
4. An ethos is transferable, not dying with a person or even a generation.

Notice, I am not offering you a four-step process to create an ethos. All I am offering, in retrospect, is four principles that might help you create your own guiding ethos.

First, an ethos is a compilation of ideals/values that one has already lived. Many believe the written Navy SEAL ethos has been around a long time. Not so. After speaking with a few individuals and friends in the know, I discovered that many aspects of their ethos had been an unspoken or taught belief before it was ever placed on paper. Danny Dietz lived by those values; only later would those values be recorded in one official document. Around 2007 the naval special warfare community began the process of placing these long-held beliefs and values on paper. From there, titled "Forged by Adversity," it became the official ethos of the United States Navy SEALs.

For my family, we have been living the values we put down on paper, or attempting to live, in some cases for decades. My wife and I have been learning about most of the statements in our family ethos for decades. They are tried-and-true principles that serve as a guidance for successful and healthy living. For us, it was just the time for our daughters and for us parents to place these in written form and begin living them outward in a stronger manner.

In short, we did not have to think long and hard about what belonged in the ethos. We already knew. I literally sat down with a piece of paper and wrote down bullet point statements based upon our faith. I started with what I know to be true about living. I then took some time to think about that which I aspired to live. This leads us to the second principle I stumbled upon.

Secondly, an ethos is something that drives and pushes one forward. Early in the book I shared that a twenty-six-year veteran of the Navy SEAL program labeled Danny as the "consummate SEAL." As previously written, it is not unusual to visit memorial pages and see other Navy SEAL teammates label Danny as "quintessential." Why? For them, he was the ultimate picture of this special warrior, in part based upon his foundational adherence to the values and ideals Navy SEALs uphold.

Value statements are one thing; an ethos is something different. Value statements talk about what you believe is significant. An ethos states, "This is what drives me, drives us. This is our foundation, and from it we shall never move."

In looking at our family, I simply asked, "What kind of people do we want to be, to become?" This is almost a dangerous question. The question forces us to examine where we are, or maybe where we are not, in our lives. This led me to the third principle.

Thirdly, an ethos calls us to a larger life. Have you read the Navy SEAL ethos? During the work of this book, I have probably read the SEAL ethos a hundred times. So many times while reading it I caught myself thinking, *Wow. There are people who actually breathe this, walk this, and live this. Amazing.* And amazing it is indeed. Many young recruits coming into the program today are motivated to live this larger life by the nature of the ethos itself. The virtue is already within. The document helps bring that to the forefront as a daily walk.

A true ethos that drives a person will force them into the situational crossroads of "Either I can live life greater, larger, and more free—or I can go home to the status quo." And when I am gone from this world, I want to know that I left to my daughters a greater way of viewing and living life.

Fourthly, an ethos is transferable, not dying with a person or even a generation. In so many ways the Holy Scriptures is an ethos—truth statements that foundation a life, pushing us to live greater than where we currently reside. The Scriptures are and have been transferable through the generations. An ethos in general is something that potentially can be passed from generation to generation. Why? An ethos contains or is based upon truth statements. Truth statements are timeless, never need changing, and weather the fashion and trend of a current society.

A true ethos can steady the resolve of its followers, because the followers know that whatever may come, whatever forces may come against them, their ethos remains firm. Returning to some of the essays, we have to dig deep within at times to weather that which we may face.

I close with previously quoted words from the book of Matthew in narrative form. Nearly two years ago, while on business in California, I had the honor of visiting the Ronald Reagan Library and Museum. I stood at his grave, visited the Oval Office replica, and looked through the numerous exhibits. Yet the signature book from the funeral of the fortieth president is what brought me to tears. There the pages were opened to a signature by his longtime friend and the former British Prime Minister Margaret Thatcher: "Well done, thou good and faithful servant." May we live an ethos-driven life, worthy to be labeled with such words.

Dan's letter to Danny after his death…

I wonder what went through his mind as his life slipped away. Until you value yourself you will not value your time, you will not do anything with it. I wonder what was going through his mind as he lay their dying. Was he thinking of his sister or his brother? Was his mother standing by his side still watching over him, protecting him saying it's alright? You've done your duty. You have lived up to more than your expectation; you have done what you have always done all your short life, protecting your little sister and your little brother, your brothers in arms. You have not backed down; you have faced the ultimate, most sacred place an individual can go. You have done well my son. When you were a little boy, I could not have imagined the character that you displayed as I look back. I think to myself, I wish it could have been me instead of you. But then again, would it be him grieving or suffering and would that be selfish of me to put that on you. You are in glory, at rest, at peace. I cannot take that away from you. The legacy you have left is far from what my little imagination could have come up with. Your display of courage was from deep within. It is who you are; your idea was far above mine. It was at a level I couldn't even have imagined. To see that is the Eye of Nobility!

You shrugged off your wounds continued to go on and on with wound after wound and still cling to life. It was what you believed my son. Your strength, your will to live, was to insure that your brothers were protected. You were not thinking of yourself, you were trying to eliminate the threat of harm. That my son is true courage! That is the type of courage that very few can display, or even imagine. Giving the Ultimate Sacrifice for your family, your home, and your country. Trusting the ones left behind to take care of the responsibility for which you thought so sacred. Danny you'll forever remain young. While the ones that remain behind will grow old. You have accomplished what others that live to in their 80's have never reached. Son if I had just one more day with you!!!

Love your Dad....

Endnotes

1   (Exodus 3:5)

2   Lincoln, Abraham. "The Gettysburg Address." Voices of Democracy. (November 1863) http://voicesofdemocracy.umd.edu/lincoln-gettysburg-address-speech-text/

3   Bobby Dall, Rikki Rocket, Bruce Anthony Johannesson, Bret Michaels. "Something to Believe In." Cyanide Publishing, 1986

4   C.S. Lewis. "A Grief Observed." HarperOne, 2009

5   (Isaiah 6:8)

6   (Isaiah 6:8)

7   Churchill, Winston. http://www.brainyquote.com/quotes/quotes/w/winstonchu130619.html

8   http://www.military.com/military-fitness/navy-special operations/navy-seal-grinder-pt

9   www.wallbuilders.com

10   Bruce, Ed. "Mammas Don't Let Your Babies Grow Up to be Cowboys." United Artists Records. 1976

11   www.militarytimes.com/valor/navy-gunners-mate-2nd-class-seal-danny-p-dietz/958396

12   www.facebook.com/pages/danny-dietz-memorial-page

13   Sun Tzu. "The Art of War: Classic Edition." Special Edition Books; Reprint edition. June 1, 2009.

14   Confucius.   http://www.beliefnet.com/Quotes/
      Inspiration/C/Confucius/Humility-Is-The-Solid-
      Foundation-Of-All-The-Virtue.aspx

15   http://www.catholiceducation.org/articles/religion/
      re0015.html

16   (Micah 6:8)

17   (Matthew 5:14)

18   Winthrop, John. "A Model of Christian Character."
      Religious Freedom. 1630. http://religiousfreedom.
      lib.virginia.edu/sacred/charity.html

19   http://www.merriam-webster.com/dictionary/
      intelligence

20   www.facebook.com/pages/
      danny-dietz-memorial-page

21   Bush, George W. George W. Bush's Remarks at His
      Presidential Library Dedication (Text). The New
      York Times. April 26, 2013. http://www.nytimes.
      com/2013/04/26/us/politics/george-w-bushs-
      remarks-at-his-presidential-library-dedication.
      html?pagewanted=all&_r=0

22   (Proverbs 22:1)

23   http://militarytimes.com/valor/navy-gunners-
      mate-2nd-class-seal-danny-p-dietz/958396

24   Sun Tzu. "The Art of War: Classic Edition." Special
      Edition Books; Reprint edition. June 1, 2009.

25   Jefferson, Thomas.   Quotation to Peter Carr.
      Quotations on Education. http://www.monticello.
      org/site/jefferson/quotations-education

26   Socrates. Goodreads - Quotable Quotes. http://
      www.goodreads.com/quotes/9431-the-only-true-
      wisdom-is-in-knowing-you-know-nothing

27   Swindoll, Chuck. Goodreads - Quotable Quotes.
      http://www.goodreads.com/quotes/313428-we-are-
      all-faced-with-a-series-of-great-opportunities

28   Jefferson, Thomas. To Edward Everett. Quotations
      on Education.   http://www.monticello.org/site/
      jefferson/quotations-education

29   Plutarch. Quotations Book. http://quotationsbook.
      com/quote/13801/#sthash.uqtRw6Jb.dpbs

30   Plutarch. Quotations Book. http://quotationsbook.
      com/quote/13801/#sthash.uqtRw6Jb.dpbs

31   Carter, Wanda Hope. "To Achieve Your Dreams
      Remember Your ABCs." 1991. http://www.inspi-
      rationmotivation.com/art/posters/to_achieve_your_
      dreams_remember_your_abcs_4th_edition_poster_
      with_shooting_star_background

32   Marshall, Crista. "Navy Cross Awarded to Littleton
      Man." The Denver Post. September 2006.   http://
      www.denverpost.com/frontpage/ci_4331954

33   Paine, Thomas. ThinkExist. Thomas Paine Quotes.
      http://thinkexist.com/quotation/reputation_is_
      what_men_and_women_think_of_us/149842.html

34   Rohn, Jim. Leading an Inspired Life. http://www.
      jimrohn.com/leading-an-inspired-life-by-jim-rohn.
      html

35   Collins   Dictionary.   www.collinsdictionary.com/
      dictionary/english/steadfastness

36   Free   Dictionary.www.thefreedictionary.com/
      indomitable

37   Jeremiah, David. Sanctuary: Finding Moments of Refuge in the Presence of God. Thomas Nelson, 336. September 2011.

38   Chapman, Beth Nielsen. Recorded by Willie Nelson. "A Horse Called Music." Columbia. 1989

39   Museum of Leadership. Annual Message to Congress. December 1, 1862 by Abraham Lincoln. http://www.leadershipnow.com/museum/AbrahamLincolnSpeeches.html

40   Edison, Thomas. Brainey Quote. http://www.brainyquote.com/quotes/quotes/t/thomasaed132683.html

41   The Churchill Centre and Museum at the Churchill War Rooms, London. Quotes FAQ. Speech given October 29, 1941. http://www.winstonchurchill.org/learn/speeches/quotations/quotes-faq

42   Roosevelt, Theodore. "The Strenuous Life: Essays and Addresses" Dover Thrift Additions. 257. Dover Publications. 2009

43   Luttrell, Marcus. "The Lone Survivor." Little, Brown, and Company. May 2009

44   (Psalm 61:3)

45   Danny Dietz Memorial Page. www.facebook.com/pages/danny-dietz-memorial-page

46   Best Wise Words. Wisdom Quote, Napoleon Bonaparte. http://www.bestwisewords.com/quote/1061/the-truest-wisdom-is-a-resolute-determination.html

47   (Psalm 27:1)

48   ThinkExist. Virgil Quotes. http://thinkexist.com/quotation/his_resolution_is_unshaken-tears-though_shed/345295.html

49   (Psalm 61:1-3)

50   Churchill, Winston. "Where Do We Stand?" House of Commons. August 16, 1945. http://www.ibiblio. org/pha/policy/1945/1945-08-16c.html

51   The Official Website of Arlington National Cemetery. "The Tomb of the Unknowns." http:// www.arlingtoncemetery.mil/visitorinformation/ TombofUnknowns.aspx

52   Danny Dietz Memorial Page. www.facebook.com/ pages/danny-dietz-memorial-page

        Arlington National Cemetery.

53   Bunch, Joey. "Ultimate Sacrifice Will Not Be Forgotten." The Denver Post. July 2005   http:// www.denverpost.com/frontpage/ci_2861708

54   (John 15:13)

55   Bush, George W.   Remarks to the Reserve Officers Association.   October 2006.   http://con- nection.ebscohost.com/c/speeches/22927342/ remarks-reserve-officers-association

56   Treptow, Martin.   Arlington National Cemetery. www.ArlingtonNationalCemetery.net. The American Presidency Project.

57   Reagan, Ronald.   "Remarks at a United States - France Ceremony Commemorating the 40th Anniversary of the Normandy Invasion, D-Day, June 6, 1945."   http://www.reaganfoundation.org/tgcde- tail.aspx?p=TG0923RRS&h1=0&h2=0&sw=&lm=r eagan&args_a=cms&args_b=1&argsb=N&tx=1742

58   Kennedy, John F. Inaugural Address. January, 1961. http://www.presidency.ucsb.edu/ws/?pid=8032

59   George W. Bush.   Press Gaggle by Tony Snow.
        http://www.presidency.ucsb.edu/ws/?pid=60286

60   Bunch, Joey.   "Ultimate Sacrifice Will Not Be
        Forgotten." The Denver Post. July 2005   http://
        www.denverpost.com/frontpage/ci_2861708

61   Magee Jr., John Gillespie.   "High Flight."
        August   1941.   http://en.wikipedia.org/wiki/
        John_Gillespie_Magee,_Jr.

62   (Hosea 13:14)

63   (Isaiah 40:31)

64   (Isaiah 40:28-31)

65   Dictionary.com   http://dictionary.reference.com/
        browse/ethos